YOUR CHILD WILL GET WELL FASTER
WHEN YOU DISCOVER THE PRACTICAL
ANSWERS TO THESE COMMON QUESTIONS:

- How safe are over-the-counter remedies?

- How do I know if my child really needs medicine?
  Don't some ailments just go away by themselves?

- How do I resume medication after missing a dose?

- What are the easiest ways to administer medication
  to a child?

- Is there specific information I should know when I
  buy and use prescription medicines?

Written for parents by health-care professionals,
Children's Medicine will arm you with all the facts
you need to make an informed choice at the drug
counter—and to make sure your child gets the best
medication possible.

CHILDREN'S MEDICINE

ANN KEPLER is editor-in-chief of Budlong Press, a medical publisher
that provides patient-information materials to physicians. She is the
former managing editor of *Consumer Guide*'s medical books.

JAMES KEPLER has coauthored several books on health-related
topics.

IRA SALAFSKY, M.D., assistant professor of pediatrics at
Northwestern University School of Medicine, is an attending physician
at Chicago's Children's Memorial Hospital and at Evanston Hospital.

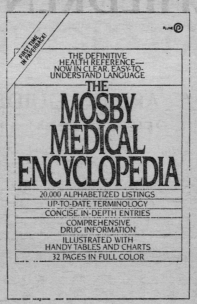

CHILDREN'S MEDICINE

A PARENT'S GUIDE TO PRESCRIPTION AND OVER-THE-COUNTER DRUGS

by

**Ann and James Kepler
with Ira Salafsky, M.D.**

A SIGNET BOOK

NEW AMERICAN LIBRARY

NAL BOOKS ARE AVAILABLE AT QUANTITY DISCOUNTS
WHEN USED TO PROMOTE PRODUCTS OR SERVICES.
FOR INFORMATION PLEASE WRITE TO PREMIUM MARKETING DIVISION.
NEW AMERICAN LIBRARY. 1633 BROADWAY.
NEW YORK. NEW YORK 10019.

Published by arrangement with Contemporary Books, Inc.
The Contemporary Books edition was published simultaneously
in Canada by Beaverbooks, Ltd., 195 Allstate Parkway,
Valleywood Business Park, Markham, Ontario L3R 4T8.

SIGNET TRADEMARK REG. U.S. PAT. OFF. AND FOREIGN COUNTRIES
REGISTERED TRADEMARK—MARCA REGISTRADA
HECHO EN CHICAGO. U.S.A.

SIGNET, SIGNET CLASSIC, MENTOR, ONYX, PLUME, MERIDIAN
and NAL BOOKS are published by New American Library,
1633 Broadway, New York, New York 10019

First Signet Printing, January, 1987

1   2   3   4   5   6   7   8   9

PRINTED IN THE UNITED STATES OF AMERICA

CONTENTS

AN IMPORTANT NOTE TO PARENTS

Every effort has been made to present the information in *Children's Medicine: A Parent's Guide to Prescription and Over-the-Counter Drugs* in the most accurate manner. However, this book is not intended to take the place of your doctor or pharmacist. Different people—and this applies especially to children—may react differently to the same medication, course of treatment, or procedure. Always consult your doctor before undertaking any course of treatment or drug therapy with your child.

Neither the authors, the consultant, nor the publisher take responsibility for any potential consequences following any action, procedure, or administration of medication by anyone reading and following the suggestions in this book. Drug research and developments change constantly in the pharmaceutical industry, and you are urged to consult your physician, pharmacist, or other health care professional for the latest advice on specific subjects or drugs.

The inclusion of a drug or product, either prescription or nonprescription and listed by either brand name or generic name, does not constitute an endorsement of that drug or product. Conversely, the exclusion of a drug or product is not a statement that that drug or product is ineffective or unsafe. Space and the scope of this book necessarily limit the number of products included.

Many medications and household items are dangerous to children, and your child may accidentally swallow a harmful substance. Also, some medications and foods react adversely with one another. Even a very young child can ingest a toxic substance or have an allergic reaction. Find out what to do now—before an emergency occurs. Turn now to Chapter 3 and read about poisons.

PART I

CHILDREN'S MEDICINE

1

HOW TO USE
THIS BOOK

As a parent or prospective parent, you have probably wondered about questions such as these:

- When can I give my child an over-the-counter remedy?
- How do I decide on the dosage?
- What questions should I ask the doctor about my child's prescription?
- How can I recognize side effects my child might develop from prescription or nonprescription medicines?
- How can I tell if my child has swallowed something he or she shouldn't have?
- How do I know if my child really needs medicine? Don't some ailments just go away by themselves?
- What should I keep on hand to take care of my child?
- How can I find out if drugstore patent remedies are any good?
- Is there specific information I should know when I buy and use prescription medicines?

At some time or another, every parent faces the task of caring for a sick child. If the illness is minor, the parent may simply deal with it at home. When the problem is more serious, however, the parent generally turns to a physician or other health care professional for help. In either case, the parent must often administer medications, and his or her ability to make sensible decisions about drugs—either non-prescription or prescription—may mean the difference between the child's uneventful recovery and a prolonged illness.

Children's Medicine is a parent's guide to medications for children. It consists of two sections: general information about giving your child medications followed by a series of profiles of specific and commonly used prescription and over-the-counter (OTC) medicines. The latter section contains notes on dosage forms and strengths, facts about signs of possible overdose, and other information.

Within the following pages, you'll find answers to questions ranging from "How much aspirin should I give?" to "How will I know if my child is having a bad reaction to a prescription?" The goal is to provide you, as a parent, with enough facts to become a responsible, knowledgeable, and effective caregiver to your child.

Perhaps, like most parents, you often use over-the-counter remedies to treat your child's minor illnesses. Generally, about the only guidance you get on a regular basis regarding these products is advertising claims. Just how accurate are they? The best way to find out is to ask questions of your doctor and your pharmacist. Some remedies are very helpful, and some are simply not worth the expense. Check the guidelines provided in Chapters 2 and 6 for selecting medicine cabinet supplies and OTC preparations, and then, before making a purchase, discuss the product with your druggist. (Don't rely on the opinions and personal experiences of the drugstore clerk, by the way. Talk to a registered pharmacist; he or she has been trained specifically to know the composition and actions of drugs. Even OTC preparations can cause serious problems if used incorrectly.)

Many widely advertised OTC medications (also called *patent remedies*) may provide slight relief of minor symptoms, but their overall effectiveness is minimal. A few can even do more harm than good. Perhaps some of the medicines that your own parents used to treat you when you weren't well are still on the market and selling well. That fact alone, however, does not mean that those products are either effective or entirely safe.

You should always check with either your doctor or your pharmacist before giving your child any kind of OTC remedy. There is no point in wasting your money, and you certainly don't want to risk making your child's condition worse than it already is. If a product with which you are familiar is not listed in Part II of this book, ask a health care professional's advice before buying it. It could be that the item does not measure up to its advertised claims, or perhaps there is another, more beneficial product that would do the job better, faster, or cheaper. Of course, with the hundreds of products on the market, one item's omission from the profile list does not mean that it is ineffective or harmful.

Because not all medications are used to treat or cure illness—some are designed to prevent illness—Chapter 4 tells you how to keep your child healthy. It will give you important tips about vitamin and mineral supplements as well as immunization facts and schedules.

Aspirin and aspirin substitutes are the most commonly used OTC medications and you will find an entire separate chapter (Chapter 5) devoted to those drugs. It includes a chart explaining proper dosages and tells you why basing your child's aspirin dosage on his or her weight rather than age is safer and more accurate.

Prescription drugs, by their very nature, are used under a doctor's orders. Nevertheless, the more you understand about prescription drugs, the more likely it is that you will be able to comply knowledgeably with your doctor's instructions. Research has shown that many persons, upon leaving their doctor's office, do not fully understand what the doctor has told them about using a prescribed drug. When you turn to Chapter 7, you will see how to read a prescription and how to have it filled. Included is a list of questions to ask your doctor before giving your child any prescription drug. And keep in mind that there is nothing at all wrong with asking your physician if your child really needs a prescribed medication.

Whether you are treating your child with over-the-counter or prescription medications, you will need to know how to administer various forms of drugs. If your child is not able to swallow a tablet or capsule, what can you do? Eardrops dribble out of your child's ears—how can you prevent it? How can you accurately measure liquid medicine so that your child does not get too much? Chapter 8 will help you with these problems and explain exactly how you can help your child get well faster by following instructions carefully.

Being aware of and coping with possible drug side effects is also your responsibility as a parent treating a sick child. But which side effects are minor and expected, and which are serious adverse reactions? When can you handle a minor side effect, and when should you call your doctor? Chapter 9 will help you become alert to both major and minor drug reactions as you treat your child's illness. Knowing what to watch for is an important part of assessing the effectiveness of the treatment process.

There are some common problems that you as a parent will confront many times over. Can you treat problems such as fever, diarrhea, and diaper rash at home, or should you call the doctor? If you do use home remedies, which ones work best? Chapter 10, which deals with the treatment of common problems, provides guidelines for preventing and handling a variety of normal, ordinary childhood ailments.

The profiles of drugs—both prescription (Chapter 11) and over-the-counter (Chapter 12)—that are commonly used for treating children's illnesses are arranged alphabetically in Part II of this book for easy reference. Check them for warnings regarding specific medications as well as storage and administration tips, side effect and overdose symptoms, and helpful precautions and suggestions. The profiles of OTC products also include recommended dosages.

Remember that all drugs are chemicals. Before you allow your child to consume chemicals, you should learn all you can about them. The purpose of this book is to help you do just that. Don't hesitate to ask questions of your physician, pharmacist, or any other health care professional. It's important that you learn all you can about your child's medicine so that you can use it most effectively to heal, not to harm.

2

STOCKING YOUR MEDICINE CABINET

Two rules of thumb to keep in mind when stocking your home's medicine cabinet are (1) keep it safe and (2) keep it simple. Simplicity, readiness, and accessibility are what you're looking for.

MEDICATIONS

The simplest and safest medicine cabinet need contain only three medications: aspirin, aspirin substitute, and syrup of ipecac.

Aspirin and Aspirin Substitutes

Regular adult strength aspirin (Bayer, St. Joseph's, and others), sometimes labeled *acetylsalicylic acid* or *ASA* for short, comes in only one strength: 5 grains per tablet. The strength may also be expressed in milligrams as 325 mg per tablet. Children's aspirin is one-fourth the strength of regular, or adult, tablets: 1¼ grains, or 80 milligrams, per tablet.

Aspirin substitute is called *acetaminophen* and is sold under the trade names Tylenol, Panadol, and so on. The strength of each tablet, adults', or children's, is expressed similarly to aspirin, that is, 5 grains (325 mg) per regular tablet and 1¼ grains (80 mg) per children's tablet.

7

Both aspirin and acetaminophen are used to treat pain and fever, but aspirin has an additional effect against inflammation, the redness, heat, and soreness that appear around cuts, bruises, and damaged tissues. Aspirin substitute may help ease some of the pain of inflammation but will do little to relieve the redness. Neither product will kill any germs that may be helping to cause some of the inflammation.

Syrup of Ipecac

Syrup of ipecac (no trade names—that's what it's called on the label) is a liquid made from the dried root of a South American plant. The primary use of ipecac is to cause vomiting, generally after a person has swallowed certain kinds of strong or poisonous liquids, powders, or other substances. Ipecac is given by the tablespoon to make a person, usually a child, throw up the harmful substance.

Caution: Turn now to Chapter 3 and read about poisons. Making a child vomit after he or she has swallowed some kinds of poisons may be the worst possible thing you can do. Ipecac is useful only in those cases when the recommended first action is to cause vomiting. At other times ipecac may also be considered a dangerous substance because of the reaction it produces. Check Chapter 3 now to see when vomiting should and should not be a first-aid treatment.

With aspirin, aspirin substitute, and syrup of ipecac on hand, you're ready to begin adding other medicines, preparations, and useful items to your medicine cabinet. Some handy additions are described below.

Alcohol

Buy the kind that says *rubbing alcohol* or *isopropyl alcohol* on the label. The strength will be about 70%, which means the alcohol has been mixed with water to make a diluted solution. Alcohol has mild antiseptic properties and is useful for wiping off thermometers or other surfaces where germs might grow. It also is a good rubbing compound for aching muscles. Isopropyl alcohol should be used only externally— never swallowed. It is flammable, so it should not be used around open flames, including lighted cigarettes.

Hydrogen Peroxide

Peroxide is sold in strengths of 3% or less, as stated on the label. It is handy to have when cleaning minor cuts and scrapes because of its foaming action. At times when it may not be possible to clean out a break in the skin thoroughly with soap and water because of tenderness around the area, a little peroxide poured directly into the wound will fizz up and lift dirt particles out of the cut. (This cleansing may sting slightly, but the discomfort passes quickly.)

Peroxide should not be used for deep or puncture wounds or badly burned areas, as it can cause irritation. These wounds need medical attention.

Peroxide is sold in brown bottles to protect it from light and should be stored in a closed cabinet away from light; it loses its strength when exposed to light.

Calamine Lotion

Calamine lotion is a mixture of a fine, white clay called *kaolin* and water that makes a soothing lotion for application to skin rashes. Sometimes zinc oxide is added to the mixture. Calamine lotion helps stop the itching of poison ivy, poison sumac, and chicken pox. As it dries it forms a powdery white coating over the skin. Don't use calamine lotion on areas where the skin is broken, and never apply it over raw, weeping, or crusting sores on the skin. Calamine lotion separates quickly, so the bottle should be recapped and shaken periodically as the lotion is being applied.

Petroleum Jelly

Vaseline is a popular brand of petroleum jelly; many stores also carry their own brand—either is acceptable. It is a very thick, greasy, whitish jelly that has excellent protective and lubricating qualities. Petroleum jelly soothes minor skin irritations and dry hands. Use it to lubricate the tip of a rectal thermometer for easy and painless insertion. Don't use petroleum jelly on any rubber items or surfaces because it will corrode them.

K-Y Jelly

K-Y is a brand name for a water-soluble lubricating jelly. The biggest advantage it has over petroleum jelly as a lubricant is that it can easily be removed from surfaces—especially handy when lubricating a thermometer—because it washes off with cold water, thereby reducing the possibility of harming the thermometer. Neither K-Y Jelly nor petroleum jelly has any germ-killing properties.

Iodine Solution

Buy a nonstinging solution such as Betadine. Iodine is only slightly more effective than soap and water for cleaning minor wounds, but it does have some helpful antibacterial properties. Iodine and iodine solutions are poisonous; keep them away from children. Incidentally, don't waste your money on tincture of Merthiolate or Mercurochrome; the FDA calls these drugs neither safe nor effective.

Suntan Lotion

Check the labels and use a sunscreen that contains para-aminobenzoic acid, abreviated *PABA*. Lotions, sprays, and creams that don't contain this ingredient are of little use. However, PABA can interact with some drugs. If your doctor has prescribed or suggested any medications for your child, ask his or her advice before using a PABA sunscreen for your child.

Zinc Oxide Ointment

Desitin is an example of a zinc oxide compound. Most such compounds form a protective, waterproof coating over the skin. They are particularly useful for preventing or treating diaper rash and other minor skin problems.

Nose Drops

Nose drops containing either phenylephrine hydrochloride or oxymetazoline (Neo-Synephrine and Afrin are examples) may be useful in reducing nasal stuffiness and runny nose.

They work by constricting the blood vessels inside the nose to prevent their swelling, thereby blocking nasal passages, and to prevent their secreting fluids. Nose drops should be used only for a few days, though, because they soon (after three days or so) begin tiring the constricting vessels to the point of relaxation, after which constriction ceases and secretion begins again at an even greater rate, making the original condition worse than ever. The strength of nose drops is indicated as a percentage of the active ingredient they contain, usually from ¼% (0.25%) to 1% (1.00%). Use the lower concentration for younger children.

With these basic medications in your medicine cabinet, you're reasonably well equipped to handle most minor childhood illnesses. Automatically adding such preparations as antihistamines and oral decongestants is expensive and probably not worth the cost or the bother because they have not been proved to be effective in every case of illness. Some antihistamines also produce unwanted side effects such as elevated blood pressure and blood vessel constriction. In most cases, then, the possible temporary relief of minor symptoms is not sufficient to justify either the expense or the risk of an unwanted reaction to these types of medications. In most cases, however, the effect and action of a decongestant or antihistamine may help relieve troublesome symptoms. Even so, they are not standard items to be stocked in your medicine chest.

Other medications, such as antibiotic ointments and first-aid creams, have not been shown to be much more effective than soap and water for cleansing wounds; the simple list of medications outlined above should be a sufficient basis for a well-equipped family medicine cabinet.

OTHER SUPPLIES

Naturally, you will need other supplies from time to time in addition to medications. Again, however, the list can be kept short. You will probably find it helpful to stock your cabinet with some or all of the following.

Thermometers

There are basically two kinds of thermometers: oral and rectal. It's a good idea to have one of each on hand. You can tell the difference between the two kinds by looking at the mercury chamber end of the thermometer. Rectal thermometers have rounded, bulbous ends, and oral thermometers have elongated, more pointed ends. Never attempt to take a rectal temperature with an oral thermometer; you could harm your child.

Both kinds of thermometers work the same way. Your child's body temperature causes the mercury in the instrument to expand and rise through a calibrated tube.

Thermometers are made of glass and should be stored in the cases that come with them to prevent breakage. You should take care to clean your thermometer properly and to protect it from excessive heat. To clean a thermometer, wash it off with soap and cold water, rinse it well under cold water, and then wipe it off with an alcohol-soaked cotton ball. Never wash it with warm or hot water, and never attempt to sterilize it by boiling it. Any heat more than a few degrees above normal body temperature will cause the mercury to rise to the very top of the tube and to "break." You can tell if that has happened by looking at the column of mercury. If you see any gaps in the column, that indicates the instrument is no longer serviceable; discard it.

Recently battery-powered electronic thermometers have appeared on the market. They consist of a hand-held case attached by a slender cord to a probe. The probe is used in the same way as a regular thermometer, and the temperature is read by pressing a button on the case to display a digital readout in a small window next to the button. These thermometers are accurate, easy to use, and take a shorter length of time to obtain a reading; however, they are considerably more expensive than regular instruments.

Temperature strips are also now being sold in drugstores. They are flexible plastic strips that, when held

Text continues on next page

against a child's forehead for a minute or so, give a digital
indication of the child's temperature. Heat from the child's
body causes numerals to appear on the strip. The forehead
temperature must then be matched against a scale be-
neath the numbers to determine the approximate internal
body temperature. If the reading indicates a fever, you then
use a regular thermometer to determine the child's exact
temperature. Although these strips are easy to use—you
can even use them while your child is sleeping—they are
not recommended because of their lack of precision.

Thermometer

Select either an oral or a rectal thermometer (it's a good
idea to have one of each), depending on the age of your
child. An oral thermometer cannot be used by a very young
child.

Vaporizer

There are two common types of vaporizers: cold mist and
hot steam. Vaporizers release a fine spray of water droplets
into the air and can provide relief for upper respiratory ailments. The moisturizing effect of the damp air helps open up
breathing passages and soothes dry, irritated throats. Most
physicians recommend cold mist vaporizers. Steam vaporizers may also be less desirable because of the risk of a child
coming into contact with the heating element.

Tweezers

Well-made, tight-gripping tweezers are handy for removing
splinters, cleaning wounds, and a variety of other uses.

Medication Measuring Spoon

This device, available in pharmacies, is shaped like a tube
to eliminate spillage and to measure liquid medicines accurately so that the amount given is a true medical teaspoon.

How to Take
Your Child's Temperature

One of the first questions you are likely to be asked by your doctor's assistant if you telephone to say your child is sick is "What's the child's temperature?" Be ready to report an accurate figure before you call the doctor.

Before using a thermometer, you must first shake it down; that is, you must return all the mercury to the storage bulb on the end of the instrument. Do this by tightly grasping the opposite end of the thermometer and shaking it sharply three or four times. After doing this, slowly rotate the thermometer between your thumb and fingers until you can see a short column of mercury rising from the storage bulb. Make sure the column has not yet risen into the calibrated zone of the tube.

To take an oral temperature, cleanse the thermometer, place it under your child's tongue, and instruct the child to keep it in place with his or her mouth closed for a minimum of three minutes. Don't try to take an oral temperature if your child is too young to follow instructions accurately—even if he or she objects to having his or her temperature taken rectally. In all likelihood you will not get an accurate reading. Also, don't attempt to take your child's temperature orally if he or she has a stuffy nose because the temptation to breathe through the mouth will be too great.

To take a rectal temperature, cleanse the thermometer, lubricate it with a little Vaseline or K-Y Jelly, and insert it an inch or two into the rectum. Hold it in place for at least two minutes. Keep your hand on the child to prevent him or her from rolling over onto the thermometer or making a sudden move that could either dislodge the thermometer or break it. The best way to take an infant's temperature is to lay the baby face down across your knees, insert the thermometer into the rectum, and

text continues on next page

hold it in place by cupping your hand over the baby's bottom with the thermometer held between two fingers. Place your other hand on the baby's back or shoulders to hold him or her quietly.

Another way to take a child's temperature is to place a thermometer in his or her armpit for about 10 minutes. This method is not recommended, however, because of its relative inaccuracy.

After you have held the thermometer in place long enough (a minimum of three minutes for oral tempera- ture, two minutes for rectal), remove the thermometer and read it by slowly rolling it between your fingers as described above. Your child's temperature is indicated by the extension of the column of mercury. Carefully note the exact point on the calibrated scale where the column stops. Each mark between two numbers stands for two- tenths of a degree. Measure the temperature by observ- ing the two numbers between which the mercury column stops and counting the tenths beyond the lower number. Write down the reading so that you can take it to the telephone with you when you call the doctor.

Thermometers are marked in either Fahrenheit or centigrade degrees. Normal oral temperature is 98.6°F or 37°C; normal rectal temperature is 99.6°F or 37.6°C. A temperature two or more degrees above normal may be considered a fever.

Because ordinary kitchen teaspoons come in such a variety of shapes and sizes, you should never use one when measuring liquid medicines.

First-Aid Items

It's unlikely that your child will escape the inevitable cuts and scrapes of childhood. You should keep gauze rolls and sterile pads, adhesive tape, and small adhesive bandages on hand for such occasions; a few cloth strips can also be handy for securing bandages.

First-Aid Manual

Buy an easy-to-understand, indexed first-aid guide and read it at your leisure before you encounter an emergency. It is nerve-wracking to search frantically through unfamiliar instructions with a crying, bleeding child on your lap.

TRAVEL MEDICINE KIT

You might want to keep a packed medicine kit on hand and ready for traveling. Constructing such a kit before you actually prepare for a trip lessens the possibility of your omitting specific items. Also, it serves as a reserve supply of staple items in the event you run out at home. In making up your kit, mark the date on those items that may deteriorate with age (aspirin and peroxide, for example) so that you will know when to replace them with fresh supplies. Never put travel supplies of any medication, prescription or OTC, into unmarked containers.

Include the three basic medicine cabinet medications in your travel kit: aspirin, aspirin substitutes, and syrup of ipecac. Consider where you might be traveling and add whatever other items you feel are important to have on hand. For vacations or longer trips, you may want to include any medications your child uses on a semi-regular basis. For example, if he or she is unusually susceptible to ear infections or recurrent skin inflammations and you are planning to travel in remote areas, you might include your doctor's recommended medication for these ailments. You may also want to discuss motion sickness medication with your doctor if your child seems prone to this affliction while traveling. Include basic first aid items; your child could be injured anywhere.

If your child is taking a prescription medication, make sure you have an adequate supply before leaving on a trip. It may be impossible to refill the prescription anywhere but your local pharmacy. Discuss this point with your doctor if you are planning an extended trip.

STORING MEDICINES SAFELY

It cannot be emphasized too strongly that the most important consideration when stocking your medicine chest is safety. Keeping the inventory up to date is a good start toward meeting this goal. Remember also to try to obtain all medicines with safety caps; however, take precautions to keep even those safety containers out of the reach of children. Other precautions include:

- Ask your doctor for specific instructions when he or she prescribes any new medication, including how it might react with over-the-counter medications. Your pharmacist is another good source of information. When you buy OTC products, tell the pharmacist what prescription medications, if any, your child is taking and ask if the product you have selected will react with them.
- Store all medications in their original containers with clearly marked labels and instructions. If you buy a new supply of an OTC product before your old container is empty, don't mix the new with the old. Some medications lose or gain strength as they age, and you won't be able to tell the new from the old if they are mixed together.
- Do not keep leftover medications unless your child takes medicine for a specific condition on a regular basis. Flush all leftover medication down the toilet and safely discard the containers. Medicine containers should not be given to children to play with. Doing so conveys the message that medicine is a toy. Also, water drunk from an empty medicine bottle might contain residue of the drug and could possibly be harmful to your child.
- Keep all medications locked away from your child. Separate adult medications from children's medicines to avoid potential confusion and be certain your child cannot gain access to either.
- Be vigilant about checking the medicine cabinet and reading expiration dates on all medications. Do not use any medication that you have kept beyond the expiration date. In some cases, the medication will no

longer be effective; in others, the preparation may have actually become more concentrated and therefore toxic over time.

Where to Store Medications

One of the poorest places to store medications is, ironically, the bathroom medicine cabinet; humidity from baths and showers can affect the composition and maybe even the potency of many drugs. In addition, most medicine cabinets are located above the sink, making it easy for an inquisitive child to climb up to reach them.

The safest place to keep medications is in a locked chest in a closet or cupboard away from both the bathroom and the kitchen. Most drugs should be stored in a cool, dry, dark spot. Lock the chest and put the key out of reach of your child. Don't let your child watch you take the key to the chest and unlock it.

If medication you are using is supposed to be kept refrigerated, don't allow it to freeze. Freezing and thawing can break down the ingredients of some drugs as well as cause tablets to crack and liquids to separate.

A properly stocked medicine chest is a must for every home. However, medication safety is also a prime consideration. To be effective and useful, your medicine cabinet should be cleaned out periodically and all drugs and supplies kept up to date.

Poison Control Centers

Check your telephone directory now for the number of the poison control center nearest you. If there is no listing, call your nearest hospital emergency room and ask for the number. Post the number on your telephone; taking this action now may save your child's life if the child accidentally swallows poison or spills a caustic substance on his or her skin.

The poison control center will likely have a toll-free 800 number. That may nor may not mean that the center is located in another city. Don't be concerned if the center is not local; it is still your best source of information concerning poisons. Occasional efforts have been made to establish a single national source for all information about poisons, but as yet the United States has no central clearinghouse for such data. Therefore, regional centers have been designated to supply vital information to hospitals, health care professionals, fire and police departments, and the general public.

If you telephone the center in an emergency and tell them, "I think my child has just swallowed poison," the first question you will be asked will be "What was it and how much did the child swallow?" Be prepared to answer by taking the container with you to the telephone. Tell the center the name of the product and the list of ingredients on the container. If the substance is a prescription medication, tell the center what it is. If you don't know, tell the center the name of the pharmacy, its telephone number, and the prescription number.

Describe any symptoms your child is exhibiting and be ready to write down whatever instructions the center gives you. You may be told how to treat the problem yourself. Or the center may instruct you to call an emergency squad or to take the child to your doctor yourself. Be certain you clearly understand each instruction, and then do exactly what you are told to do.

3

ACCIDENTAL
POISONING

One of the greatest health hazards for children is accidental poisoning. If you have any kind of medicines or strong solutions around the house—and who doesn't keep at least a few such staple products on hand?—the possibility of your child accidentally consuming poison exists in your home. Even substances that many people take for granted pose serious risks. The most common cause of poisoning in children ages one through five, for instance, is overdose of aspirin.

Of course, there are many other common, everyday substances that can poison a child—plants, insecticides, soaps, cleansers, polishes and waxes, and almost any household cleaning substance. In fact, just about any substance in large enough quantity can be toxic. How can you protect your child from accidental poisoning?

Before discussing prevention, let's look first at what could prove to be a lifesaving precaution for your child—the simple posting of a list of telephone numbers to call in the event of an emergency. Check your telephone directory for the number of a poison control center; it will most likely be a toll-free 800 number. Don't be concerned if the center is not local; it will still be your best source of information if your child swallows a life-threatening substance.

List the poison control center number along with the numbers of the police and fire departments (even if your community uses the emergency 911 call system, write it down; you could become confused in an emergency and forget it), your child's physician and your family physician, the closest hospital and pharmacy, and at least one neighbor. Write the list in ink on heavy paper (three-by-five-inch index cards are ideal) and tape a copy to the bottom of every telephone in your home. A list posted next to the telephone or in a book can be moved and therefore hard to find when you need it in a hurry. With the list actually attached to the telephone you can avoid spending precious minutes searching at a time when every second counts.

Take a few minutes right now to make and attach your lists and then inform everyone in your household about the numbers. Always make it a part of your instruction briefing to baby-sitters, household help, or anyone else who is in your home on a temporary or occasional basis. It is also a sensible precaution to leave your full name, your home address, and your home telephone number next to each phone on those occasions when a new baby-sitter or other caregiver is looking after your child. If the baby-sitter needs to call for emergency help, this information will be necessary, and a new sitter may not even know your address, especially if you picked him or her up. During the excitement and stress of an emergency, even a regular sitter could forget your name and address. A bit of planning and careful instruction could be crucial to the safety of your child and your home.

Next, carefully take stock of your home. Where do you store medicines or cleaning supplies, or indeed, anything that could be potentially dangerous to a curious, perhaps climbing, child? Take a walk through your home and examine every room, closet, and cabinet. Try to see things from the vantage point of a small child who is exploring his or her world.

- Are there cleaning supplies under the kitchen or bathroom sink?
- Have you left medicines or cosmetics sitting on top of a chest of drawers?
- Is the bathroom medicine cabinet easily accessible? Could a child climb onto the sink or countertop to reach it?
- Do you carry medications in your purse, backpack, briefcase, lunch box, or coat pocket and then leave them on a chair or table?

While you are taking this inventory of your home, try to pick what might look interesting and worth exploring to a young child. Don't forget the basement, attic, garage, storage sheds, or anyplace else that your child might get into. And don't assume anything—your infant may not be crawling yet, but he or she soon will be. Also, even school-age children should not be assumed to be past the experimenting stage.

If your home does not meet reasonable safety standards, change it. Here is a list of suggested actions you can take to ensure that your home is safe and that your children are protected from accidental poisoning:

- Go directly to your telephone directory and copy down all the important numbers you might need in an emergency. Tape them to your telephone. *Do it now while you are thinking about it*.

- Remove all poisonous substances from your child's reach. The best place to store such items is in a locked cupboard to which only you have the key. "Child-proof" cabinet locks without keys are not acceptable. Proceed from the assumption that if you can figure out how to open it so can your child.

- Do not assume that because a medicine or other substance is kept in a high place it is safe. Even a very young child can pull a chair up to a cabinet, climb up, and reach inside.

- Be certain that all medications, whether for children or adults, have "child-proof" caps. Granted, such safety caps can be frustrating to use, but they are an important factor in preventing childhood poisoning. Don't stop there, though. Many manually dexterous toddlers may be able to open a "safety" cap even more quickly than their parents can. The only safe solution is a locked cabinet.

- Always store a dangerous substance in its original container with its label intact. You may need to know precisely what ingredients are in the substance in the event of an emergency.

- Never store a medication in an unlabeled container. By all means, never store a medication in a container that originally held something edible; your child may think that medicines are safe to eat.

- There are "danger" labels available that can be placed on containers. (Ask your druggist where to find "Mr. Yuk" labels, for example, and information about how to use them.) Your child can be taught that this label means that what is inside the container is bad and that the container should not be touched.
- Never tell your child that medicine is candy or tastes like candy. Don't refer to pieces of candy such as M&Ms or fruit-flavored tablets as pills.
- Do not allow your child to watch you take medications. Most young children like to imitate their parents. Be certain also to warn regular baby-sitters or day care workers not to take medicine in front of your child.
- During stressful or active times, such as on moving day, on holidays, or when repairmen are working in your home, be sure to watch your child carefully. If you know you will be distracted or busy, you might consider arranging for a baby-sitter to look after your child.
- When you visit other homes, make certain that your child does not come into contact with poisonous substances.
- When guests visit you, see that medicines they are carrying are out of reach of your child.
- Finally, don't be the unwitting reason your child is at risk from too much medication. Purchase a medically calibrated spoon or eyedropper to administer prescribed amounts of medicine to your child. And if you miss a dose of medication, don't give two doses at once; call your doctor to find out what to do.

FIRST AID FOR POISONING

If, despite all your precautions, your child swallows a poisonous substance, what should you do? First, you must remain as calm as possible. Seconds can count, and you will be unable to help your child if you are unable to concentrate on what you're doing. Also, if you convey your excitement and fear to your child, it may make the situation worse. Your child may already be frightened, and seeing you in a state of panic will probably increase that fright. If your child is excited, his or her body will react in such a way that it could increase the harmful effect of the poison. Follow these steps:

1. If you child is unconscious, confused, experiencing severe abdominal pain, vomiting, in convulsions, or otherwise displaying acutely abnormal symptoms, *call an emergency life squad or ambulance at once*. If your child's symptoms appear less threatening, try to find out what the child has taken and when. Find the container for the substance.

2. Take the container to the telephone and call the poison control center or your doctor. Be prepared to read the label of the substance over the phone; spell the ingredients if you can't pronounce them clearly—many substance names sound alike, and it is important to report precisely what the product contains. Describe your child's symptoms. Have a pencil and paper available to write down instructions.

3. Do not induce vomiting with syrup of ipecac unless the poison control center or the doctor directs you to do so. In some cases inducing vomiting can be dangerous. As a general rule, if your child has taken a normally edible substance, including medications, induce vomiting. If he or she has consumed a normally nonedible substance, such as paint, cleaning fluid, and so on, do not induce vomiting. Do not induce vomiting—under any circumstances—if your child is not fully conscious.

4. If you are instructed to give syrup of ipecac, administer one tablespoon of the syrup (or whatever dose the poison control center specifies) followed by one-half to one full eight-ounce glass of water. Do not give milk. Your child should vomit within 10 to 15 minutes. If he or she has not vomited after 20 minutes, call the poison control center to see if you should give more syrup of ipecac.

5. If your child vomits, try to save the vomited material to take to the doctor or hospital emergency room. (A large plastic bag is handiest for this. Get one ready after you have given your child the syrup of ipecac.) Taking along vomited material can be helpful in determining what and how much poison was consumed.

6. As soon as you have completed emergency first-aid procedures, take your child to the nearest emergency room or to your doctor's office—but only if you know the doctor is in. Take the poisonous substance container and any vomited material as well. If you are too upset to drive or if your child needs constant supervision, call an ambulance or emergency life squad or the police or fire department. Give them your address as soon as you get an answer and then tell them what is wrong.

SYMPTOMS OF POISONING

There may be an occasion, unfortunately, when your child eats or drinks a poisonous substance and you will be unaware of it until telltale symptoms of poisoning or illness appear. The following symptoms should alert you to investigate the situation and call your doctor

- Aspirin overdose: rapid breathing, ringing in the ears, overexcitement, nausea, unconsciousness
- Acid or alkali poisoning: burns on the lips, mouth, or tongue
- Medication poisoning: severe abdominal pain and/or vomiting, sleepiness, lethargy
- Any symptom that is out of the ordinary should be investigated. If you have any suspicions that your child has consumed a harmful substance, call your doctor immediately.

Accidental poisoning is one childhood problem that parents can make an effort to prevent, particularly for young children. Obviously, a child's intentional overdosing on a medicine or other substance is a different situation and calls for greater measures than those necessary for physical recovery alone. A suicide attempt—and this can happen in preteen years—indicates that professional help far beyond treating the immediate symptoms of the poisoning is urgently needed.

4

KEEPING YOUR CHILD HEALTHY

One of your most important jobs as a parent is to prevent illness and to teach your children good health habits so that bouts of illness can be eliminated—or at least their number reduced. We all know that a nutritious diet, rest, exercise, and hygienic conditions help maintain good health. However, in some instances you can take more active steps to prevent illness and promote health. If you take these steps, you may be able to avoid using some medications and treatments because you have prevented the illnesses requiring such remedies.

VITAMIN AND MINERAL SUPPLEMENTS

As a general rule, vitamin and mineral supplements are not necessary for normal healthy children who are eating a balanced diet. Nevertheless, there are times when supplementation may be necessary, and you should know how to meet those needs.

Infants

If your baby is being breastfed, most of the baby's vitamin and mineral needs, with a few exceptions, will be met by the breast milk. The amount of vitamin D in breast milk, however, is insufficient to meet your baby's needs beyond the first few months of life. Therefore, all babies should receive vitamin D supplements (400 IU) every day. In addition, by the time a premature infant is two months old or a full-term infant is four to six months old, the iron reserves passed to the baby from its mother during pregnancy will be depleted. At this point, unless you are breast-feeding, you will need to add iron supplements or start the baby on dry infant cereal that is fortified with iron.

Finally, infants need fluoride supplementation to build strong teeth and bones. The best source of fluoride is fluoridated drinking water from the community water supply. Water with a fluoride level of one part per million (ppm) is considered safe and effective. If the fluoride level is below that, fluoride supplements are recommended as listed below.

The most beneficial course of action is for the child to drink fluoridated water from birth until the permanent teeth have erupted, around the age of 12 or 13 years. A word of warning, however: if the fluoride intake is excessive while the permanent teeth are coming in, the teeth's enamel may become stained and mottled. If the teeth have already erupted, this staining will not occur. You might want to contact your community's water or health department to find out exactly how much fluoride, if any, is in your community's water supply. Then you can discuss fluoride supplementation with your child's doctor. You don't want your young child to take

Concentration of Fluoride in Drinking Water

Age	<0.3 ppm	0.3–0.7 ppm	>0.7 ppm
2 wk–2 yr	0.25 mg/day	0	0
2–3 yr	0.50 mg/day	0.25 mg/day	0
2–16 yr	1.00 mg/day	0.50 mg/day	0

Source: The Committee on Nutrition of the American Academy of Pediatrics (1979).

in too much, nor do you want to deprive the child of beneficial amounts of fluoride. Remember, too, while you are deciding how much fluoride to give your child that infants and very young children, especially those being breast-fed, may not drink a great deal of water. You and your doctor should work out a supplementation level after determining the fluoride content of your water and how much water your child consumes.

Other than vitamin D, iron, and fluoride, your infant will receive sufficient vitamins and minerals in breast milk. Consult your doctor about adding a vitamin C supplement, however; some physicians feel this is also necessary. If your baby is not being breast-fed, then your prepared formula will contain the necessary supplements. If you give supplements to your child, there are liquid forms of vitamins A, C, and D (Tri-Vi-Sol with iron and fluoride, for example) that contain the preferred vitamins, iron, and fluoride. Ask your doctor about dosage. You can mix the dose with food or juice or place the drops into the baby's mouth, preferably during feeding. Never squirt a dropper of liquid directly at the baby's throat; gently release the liquid into the baby's cheek. For older children there are also chewable tablets that have both a body-wide effect and a topical effect directly on the teeth.

Older Children

Most older children who eat a balanced diet do not need supplementation. But discuss this with your doctor, who knows your child and may make specific recommendations. If you feel your child is not eating an adequate diet or for some other reason is not receiving the necessary vitamins and minerals in his or her diet, you should ask your doctor about supplementing the child's diet with vitamin and mineral tablets.

One exception to the general rule that supplements are not needed for a healthy child might be a teen-ager who is on a restricted weight-reducing diet. Many nutritionists suggest that a multivitamin preparation may be needed for those persons on diets below 1,000 to 1,200 calories per day. However, therapeutic megadoses are not necessary. Also, both you and your teen-ager should know that vitamins and minerals are not themselves sources of energy and can act only in the presence of food containing natural nutrients. Taking large doses of vitamins and minerals without eating food is therefore useless and may even be harmful.

IMMUNIZATIONS

Immunization is a method of providing artificial immunity or resistance to disease. There are two types of immunization: active and passive. An active immunization is an injection of a weak or killed virus or bacterium into the body. This stimulates the body to develop its own defenses against the virus or bacterium. Special cells produce substances called *antibodies* that are carried in the bloodstream and fight invading organisms. These antibodies remain in the body to protect it from the disease caused by the virus or bacterium in the immunization.

Passive immunization is, in effect, borrowed immunity. That is, it is an injection of ready-made antibodies most often extracted from the blood of animals that have been immunized strictly for the purpose of producing antibodies to be used in passive immunization. Passive immunization is temporary, but it does protect a person who has been infected by or exposed to an organism until the body has time to manufacture its own antibodies.

The American Academy of Pediatrics has recommended the immunization schedule in the accompanying table. This schedule protects the child against measles, mumps, rubella (German measles), polio, tetanus, diphtheria, and pertussis (whooping cough), all of which can be extremely dangerous or even fatal. The vaccination against smallpox is no longer given because, thanks to an international cooperative vaccination program, smallpox has been virtually eradicated from the world. In addition to these immunizations, your doctor will probably recommend a test for tuberculosis when your child is about one year old.

Also, in 1985 the Food and Drug Administration approved a new vaccine against *Haemophilus influenzae B* (Hib) bacteria. This immunization is recommended and is most effective for children aged two through six years. It is less effective but can be used for high-risk children as young as 18 months; unfortunately, this vaccine is ineffective for babies under 18

Immunization Schedule

Immunization	Age
DPT	2, 4, 6, 18 months, 5 years (booster)
Polio	2, 4, 18 months, 5 years
TB test	1 year
MMR	15 months
DT	14–16 years
HIB	2–6 years

Key: DPT = diphtheria, pertussis, tetanus; Polio = poliomyelitis; TB = tuberculosis; MMR = measles, mumps, rubella; DT = diphtheria, tetanus; HIB = Haemophilus influenza B.

months, and researchers are attempting to develop a vaccine for this age group. Hib bacterial infections may lead to bacterial meningitis (inflammation of the covering of the brain and spinal cord), which can cause damage to the nervous system, and/or epiglottitis (inflammation of the structure over the entrance of the voicebox), which can lead to suffocation. Hib infections can be treated with antibiotics if diagnosed in time, but it is wiser to immunize to prevent the serious complications of these infections.

Immunization Schedule

In most areas laws require that your child have these immunizations and the TB (tuberculosis) test before he or she will be allowed to enter school. Many day care facilities also require proof that a child has received or is receiving on the recommended schedule all appropriate immunizations and tests. You should be aware that a child can be refused entry to school or day care or even sent home if recommended boosters are not received.

Your physician may suggest a slightly different schedule from the one shown for your child. Also, scientific recommendations may change as other factors influence the immunization program. The vaccines against rubella, polio, and pertussis are examples.

Rubella

Although rubella is a relatively mild disease, it can be devastating to a pregnant woman, possibly causing serious long-term problems for her unborn baby. Because of this danger, a rubella vaccine was welcomed when it was introduced in 1969. At that time and ever since, the focus of this immunization has been on young babies and preschoolers. Therefore, those persons born before 1969 have probably not been immunized against rubella. In addition, those children vaccinated between 1969 and 1979 were given a vaccine that has since been found to be less effective than the one used today. Many health officials are now suggesting that attention be given to teenagers and young adults to determine—perhaps through testing—if they are immune to rubella. Some have suggested that those found to be lacking immunization be vaccinated with today's vaccine. This is especially important for girls and young women of childbearing age. (However, because the rubella vaccine uses a live virus, it should not be given to a woman who is or thinks she is pregnant. Any young woman receiving the rubella vaccine should wait at least three months after vaccination before attempting to become pregnant.)

Pertussis (Whooping Cough)

The pertussis vaccine is the *P* in the DPT immunization given to young children; the other two diseases are diphtheria and tetanus. There has been some question about the safety of the pertussis portion of the vaccine because there have been some instances of neurological damage resulting from the use of the vaccine. Because the risk of such damage following the use of the pertussis vaccine is 3.2 incidents per million doses and the risk of acquiring pertussis is 10 times that figure, most medical experts recommend the use of the vaccine. Pertussis is a serious disease, and it can kill. However, because of the safety question, some manufacturers of the vaccine stopped producing it in the mid-1980s. The result was a shortage of the vaccine. During the shortage public health officials recommended postponement of the DPT vaccinations given at 18 months and at four to six years of age until the supply of vaccine increased. Once there is a sufficient supply, those children under the age of seven years (the vaccine should not be given to anyone over seven years) should be recalled and brought up to date on the immunizations.

Polio Vaccine

There is also some question about the effectiveness of the oral polio vaccine. The oral vaccine contains a weakened, but live, polio virus. The injected vaccine contains a killed virus. Thus, use of the oral vaccine constantly introduces live weakened polio virus into the population.

Although the current practice is to use the oral vaccine, many scientists are questioning this use, even though the introduction of a live weakened virus into the population secondarily immunizes many people against polio. These scientists feel that the inactivated virus injection is safer. In the beginning, the oral vaccine had more advantages: it was easier to administer and therefore more economical. The injection was not potent enough and required multiple injections. Today, however, the injected vaccine is strong enough to provide a satisfactory immunity with just a single inoculation.

TALKING WITH YOUR DOCTOR

Both the DPT inoculation and the polio vaccine question should be discussed with your doctor. There is no widespread program to eliminate these immunizations because the diseases they prevent are more serious than the risk from the vaccines. Nevertheless, you should have all your questions answered as you embark on a vaccination schedule. Request that your doctor carefully examine your child before each shot. If your child is ill or has recently had a fever, diarrhea, or an ear infection, no vaccine should be given. Also, tell your doctor about any family history of neurological disorders, severe allergies, convulsions, or reactions to DPT vaccinations. Keep thorough records of any reaction your child has to an immunization. Often the DPT vaccination will cause your child to be fussy, sleepy, and/or feverish. These reactions should be very mild, however.

WHAT IS IN THE FUTURE?

Research is constantly going on in the field of immunizations. New techniques are being developed for manufacturing vaccines, including the use of synthetic materials and genetic engineering. Much effort is being directed toward making all vaccines safe and effective. And there are also some specific new vaccines that are being developed and tested. Within a short time there may be a vaccine against chicken pox. Scientists are also working on vaccines against meningitis, herpes simplex, malaria, and other diseases. Within your child's lifetime many diseases will become controlled or even eliminated through advanced immunization programs.

A FINAL WORD

Despite the questions about the safety and effectiveness of some of the vaccines currently being used, an immunization program is felt to be essential by almost all medical experts. You as a parent have to weigh the risk associated with the diseases and the risks of administering the vaccines for them. Most experts feel the possible risks of the vaccines are considerably lower than the risks and damage caused by these diseases. Fortunately, many of these questions may not have to be answered as scientific technology eliminates some diseases and provides safer and more effective vaccines against others.

5

ASPIRIN AND ASPIRIN SUBSTITUTES

One of the most widely used medications, aspirin is an old standby remedy for many ills and ailments. It might be considered the first "wonder drug." Developed in Germany over a century ago, it first appeared on the market in the early 1900s and has since become accepted as a popular and safe remedy for symptomatic pain and discomfort.

Parents often turn to aspirin as their first choice to relieve symptoms of their children's illnesses. Acetaminophen, the most common aspirin substitute, shares many of the same properties of aspirin and is often used in its place, especially for those who cannot tolerate aspirin. It is sold under several trade names, among them Tylenol and Panadol. A third nonaspirin pain reliever, ibuprofen, was transferred from prescription drug status to over-the-counter in 1983. Although it is not recommended for use with children under the age of 12 without a doctor's supervision, it can be used for teen-agers and in fact is especially useful in relieving menstrual cramps. It is sold over the counter as Nuprin and Advil.

Nevertheless, even with their history of usefulness and effectiveness, each of these medications still must be treated with respect. Aspirin, for instance, is the most common cause of poisoning among children between the ages of one and five years. Acetaminophen can also be very toxic in larger-than-recommended doses, and ibuprofen is not recommended for young children. Therefore, it is important for you to know when and how to use these home remedies.

HOW DO THEY WORK?

All three of these common OTC pain relievers work the same way: they inhibit the production of hormonelike substances called *prostaglandins* that trigger fever, pain, and inflammation. Aspirin fights prostaglandins that set off all three symptoms, while acetaminophen works only against those responsible for fever and pain. Ibuprofen, like aspirin, inhibits all prostaglandins, especially those in the uterus that are responsible for causing menstrual cramps.

HOW TO CHOOSE

How do you decide which pain reliever to give to your child? Before all three are examined in more detail, a rule of thumb might be helpful. Aspirin has the widest ranges of uses, but also the greatest number of side effects. Acetaminophen has the fewest number of side effects, but it is not effective against inflammation. Ibuprofen has fewer side effects than aspirin but more than acetaminophen and is also not recommended for children under the age of 12 without a doctor's supervision. A more specific look at each drug will help you develop some ground rules about when and what to use, depending on the circumstances.

ASPIRIN

Aspirin relieves pain, fever, and inflammation. It is also called *acetylsalicylic acid,* or *ASA,* a term to remember when you are reading OTC medication labels or a prescription, especially if your child is allergic to aspirin, because aspirin is sometimes contained in other compounds. Aspirin is extremely effective and the most inexpensive of the common pain relievers. It does, however, have some drawbacks.

Side Effects

A common side effect of taking aspirin is abdominal pain. Aspirin is an acid, and it can irritate the lining of the stomach. Often, however, this can be avoided if the aspirin is given along with food or milk to coat the stomach. Prolonged use and high doses of aspirin can cause stomach bleeding or interference with the blood's normal ability to clot; thus, frequent use can lead to stomach ulcers or anemia, a condition characterized by a lack of red blood cells that can result from internal bleeding. These two conditions are much more common in adults who take aspirin indiscriminately or for chronic conditions than in a child whose aspirin consumption is carefully monitored by you. The point in mentioning these serious side effects is to alert you to what can result if simple, common, everyday aspirin is not used with respect and common sense.

A small percentage of the population, especially those with asthma, have allergic reactions to aspirin. These can range from rashes and itching to choking. If your baby or child tends to be allergic—or even if he or she seems well but there is a history of allergies or asthma in your family, or you suspect the possibility of such problems in your child—discuss the use of aspirin with your doctor before administering it to your child. If an aspirin allergy exists or may exist, remember when buying other OTC products or when accepting a prescription from your doctor to check the label for the term *acetylsalicylic acid (ASA)* or to remind your doctor about the allergy.

You should also be alert for two other side effects. Ringing in the ears and rapid breathing are classic signs of aspirin overdose. Should your child display these symptoms, call your doctor immediately. If he or she is unavailable, call the poison control center.

When Should You Not Use Aspirin?

If your child is not allergic or sensitive to aspirin and does not show signs of side effects, then aspirin will probably be an effective drug for his or her minor ailments. However, even then there are some situations when the use of aspirin should be considered carefully.

Reye's Syndrome

Reye's syndrome is a rare but extremely dangerous condition that affects children and teen-agers. An inflammatory disease, it affects the brain, similarly to encephalitis, and the liver. The disease is sometimes associated with chicken pox or influenza and occurs most often during the flu season, roughly from December through March. Aspirin, when given for symptomatic relief of influenza, is thought to be a contributing factor in children's contracting Reye's syndrome. For that reason, it is always best to use an aspirin substitute (Tylenol, for example) when treating your child's flu discomfort.

Symptoms of Reye's syndrome are persistent vomiting, sleepiness, and lethargy; violent headaches; overactivity; confusion; and disorientation. Convulsions and loss of consciousness can occur as the disease progresses without treatment. Early detection and treatment are essential. Most often the victim will be hospitalized and given supportive therapy to help him or her withstand the disease until it has run its course. If your child displays symptoms of this disease, especially in association with flu, call your doctor immediately.

There is no cure for Reye's syndrome.

Reye's Syndrome. Reye's syndrome is a rare, serious, and potentially fatal condition that has been associated with chicken pox and influenza. The disease itself is a form of inflammation of the brain, or encephalitis. However, it differs from other forms of encephalitis in that the condition also involves the liver. The syndrome causes the brain to swell and the liver to accumulate fatty deposits so that neither organ can function properly. The condition must be diagnosed and treated early in order to prevent brain damage, coma, and death. Those most at risk are children between the ages of 5 and 11 (although it can strike children under 5 and even adolescents up to 18 years of age) who are recovering from a viral infection, most commonly chicken pox and influenza.

The reason you as a parent should even be aware of such a rare condition is that there are some reports of a possible link between the use of aspirin in treating a viral infection and the occurrence of Reye's syndrome. Although it has not been proven that aspirin causes Reye's syndrome, doctors and other medical professionals warn against giving aspirin to a child with a viral infection, especially the flu or chicken pox. In fact, the Food and Drug Administration has been negotiating with the aspirin industry to include such a warning on product labels, and the industry is cooperating.

You may be asking, "How will I know if my child has the flu or a viral illness? How can I tell if I can give the child aspirin?" The best rule of thumb is: when in doubt, do without. In other words, even if your child has not been diagnosed as having chicken pox or the flu by a doctor—in fact, if your child has not seen a doctor—don't use aspirin until you know the reason for your child's illness. If you do need to offer the child some symptomatic relief from pain or fever, use acetaminophen; it has not been shown to be linked to Reye's syndrome and can be used until you know what you are dealing with. In addition, as you will see below, symptomatic relief of fever is not always necessary or desirable. Therefore, using aspirin to relieve fever is not always the best treatment, especially if you are unsure of your child's diagnosis.

Mild Fever. Low-grade, or mild, fever is both a symptom and a defense mechanism. It indicates that your child's body is attempting to fight off disease. For that reason, it is not always advisable to try to lower his or her temperature; sometimes it is best just to let the fever burn itself out. Unless he or she is in apparent discomfort, exercise discretion and give your child's body a chance to take care of itself. In other words, don't be too quick to medicate. There are times when nature should be allowed to take its course without the addition of drugs. And, of course, if you have any suspicion that the cause of your child's discomfort is chicken pox or influenza, you should avoid the use of aspirin altogether.

Doctor's Visit. If your child is so sick that you decide to take him or her to see the doctor, discontinue administering aspirin immediately. Aspirin given within five hours before your child is examined by a physician can mask his or her symptoms to such an extent that it may difficult to evaluate the child's condition accurately. Naturally, if you have already given your child aspirin and then see the doctor within an hour or two, you should be certain to share that information with the doctor.

When to Use Aspirin

In the seventy or so years that aspirin has been on the market it has found wide usage as a safe and effective reliever of mild pain, particularly for headaches and toothaches. It works well in relieving muscle and joint aches and is tolerated well by most people including children. Aspirin is particularly useful for reducing fevers associated with either bacterial or viral infections.

How to Use Aspirin

Aspirin is available in several forms, the most commonly used being tablets. "Regular" tablets, that is, the adult size, have a strength of 5 grains (325 mg) per tablet, while children's tablets are one-fourth that strength, or 1¼ grains (80 mg) per tablet. Children's aspirin, in addition to having a reduced potency, is also flavored and chewable. The taste is not unpleasant, and most children will readily chew the tablet. (Regular aspirin should not be chewed; it is intended to dissolve in the stomach.)

When giving aspirin to an infant, you may want to crush the tablet and stir it into a small amount of food. The easiest way to do this is to crush the tablet between two nested spoons and then stir the resulting powder into three or four spoonfuls of pureed fruit or infant cereal. Do not use too much food. A sick baby often has little or no appetite and will refuse to eat more than three or four spoonfuls. And, of course, the baby must eat all of the food in order to receive all of the aspirin.

Older children may chew the flavored tablets, swallow them whole, or let them dissolve on the tongue. Before administering aspirin whole, be absolutely certain your child is able to swallow a whole pill or is willing to allow it to dissolve in the mouth. Also make sure your child is fully awake and alert and is not coughing and gasping; you don't

Aspirin and Acetaminophen Tablet Dosage

You may administer aspirin or acetaminophen to your child according to either weight or age. Using his or her weight is preferable for calculating an accurate dosage. Use the guidelines below. Note: this chart is for *children's-strength aspirin or acetaminophen only*—1¼ grain (80 mg) per tablet.

Age (Years)	Weight (Pounds)	Dosage
Under 2	Below 27	As directed by physician
2–3d	27–35	2 tablets
4–5	36–45	3 tablets
6–8	46–65	4 tablets
9–10	66–76	5 tablets
11 years	77–83	6 tablets
12 and over	84 and over	8 tablets

want to create a situation in which a child can choke on or inhale the tablet.

Each time you administer aspirin, follow it with at least half a glass of water, milk, or juice. Milk is recommended to help protect the stomach. Aspirin is flushed out of the body by the kidneys. It is important to observe the recommended four-hour dosage interval, so as not to overload the kidneys, and to be sure your child is drinking plenty of water to aid in the flushing process.

Dosage

Aspirin may be administered according to your child's age or weight. Using weight as a guideline when determining dosage is more effective—your three-year-old may be petite and not require or be able to tolerate the manufacturer-recommended dosage for three-year-olds. Conversely, if your three-year-old is husky or big for his or her age, the standard dose for that age may not be enough to be effective.

Aspirin Freshness

Sometimes, after repeated exposure to the air, aspirin tablets may decompose chemically, although they appear normal. Each time you open a bottle of aspirin, sniff the contents. An odor resembling vinegar indicates that the chemical composition of the aspirin has broken down and that the aspirin is not safe to use. When this happens, discard the contents by flushing the unused tablets down the toilet, and buy a new bottle. Because of aspirin's tendency to decompose rather quickly, it is often better for you to purchase small-quantity bottles rather than "economy" sizes. When it becomes necessary to throw away part of what you have bought, the per-tablet saving you thought you got by buying the larger size is lost.

Although the recommended aspirin dosage for different children may vary according to their ages and weights, the administration time interval remains the same—once every four hours—unless you are told otherwise by your doctor. You should not give your child aspirin regularly for more than five days, and you should stop altogether if the original symptoms you have been treating are not relieved within that time or if new ones appear.

If your child continues to have a low-grade fever (two or three degreees above normal) for three days or more, call the doctor. Also call the doctor if your child's symptoms include severe sore throat or headache, high fever, or nausea and vomiting. And remember: if you call the doctor for an emergency appointment, discontinue giving your child aspirin until after the doctor has seen him or her.

One further word of caution concerns the use of aspirin suppositories. The rate of absorption of the aspirin into the bloodstream is generally more uneven with the use of suppositories than with an oral administration. Therefore, the risk of aspirin poisoning is greater.

ACETAMINOPHEN

Acetaminophen is sold under the brand names Tylenol, Panadol, and others and is effective in treating fever and pain; it is not effective in reducing inflammation. It produces fewer side effects or allergic reactions than does aspirin, though on rare occasions it can cause skin rash or painful urination. High doses over an extended period of time can cause liver or kidney damage, but again this is unlikely to happen with children whose intake is being monitored. Nonetheless, because of this danger, you should never exceed recommended dosages.

When Not to Use Acetaminophen

The same guidelines apply to acetaminophen as to aspirin, with the exception of the problem of Reye's syndrome. Acetaminophen has not been linked to Reye's syndrome, and it is felt that it is safe to use during a bout of chicken pox or flu. However, as with aspirin, you may want to let a fever run its course without giving acetaminophen unless, of course, the child is extremely uncomfortable or the fever is high. Also, remember that you probably should not give acetaminophen within five hours before your child is examined by a doctor; the medication may mask the symptoms your doctor is looking for.

When to Use Acetaminophen

Acetaminophen can be used to reduce fever and relieve minor aches and pains. It probably is not quite as effective as aspirin in reducing pain and fever, but it does have fewer side effects, it is not associated with Reye's syndrome, and it can be used by those allergic or sensitive to aspirin.

How to Use Acetaminophen

Acetaminophen is available in adult-strength tablets of 5 grains (325 mg) each and in children's-strength, flavored, chewable tablets of 1¼ grains (80 mg) each. The children's

Liquid Acetaminophen Dosages

Acetaminophen is available in liquid form as drops or syrup. Administer it to your child according to age as indicated below.

Age	Drops	Syrup
0–3 months	0.4 ml	——
4–11 months	0.8 ml	½ teaspoon
1–2 years	1.2 ml	¾ teaspoon
2–3 years	1.6 ml	1 teaspoon
4–5 years	2.4 ml	1½ teaspoons
6–8 years	3.2 ml	2 teaspoons
9–10 years	4.0 ml	2½ teaspoons
11 years	4.8 ml	3 teaspoons
12 and over	3.2–6.4 ml	2–4 teaspoons

tablets can be administered in the same way as chewable aspirin tablets. (See the Aspirin Dosage chart above.) Acetaminophen is also available in a liquid (brand names Tempra and Liquiprin) form that is very convenient for infants and small children.

The tablets can be administered every four hours but not more than five times in one day unless prescribed by your doctor, in which case you should follow the doctor's instructions very carefully. Remember, an overdose of acetaminophen can lead to liver or kidney damage. If your child's fever persists more than three days, discontinue using the acetaminophen and call the doctor. If you are administering acetaminophen for pain, you should not do so for more than five days, and if new symptoms develop or any symptom persists, you should discontinue the medication and call your doctor. Severe sore throat or headache, vomiting, or high fever may be very serious symptoms indicating serious illness. Stop using acetaminophen and call the doctor.

Ibuprofen Warnings

Do not give your child ibuprofen if he or she is also taking aspirin.

Ask your doctor about ibuprofen before giving it to your child. While you are talking to the doctor, ask him or her whether buying the prescription form of this drug would be cheaper than buying the over-the-counter form. The prescription versions of ibuprofen, Motrin and Rufen, have been reduced in price by their manufacturers to compete with the OTC versions. However, the prescription formulations still contain a higher dosage of medication and, therefore, may be unsuitable for teen-agers.

IBUPROFEN

Ibuprofen is effective against fever, pain, and, like aspirin but unlike acetaminophen, inflammation. Sold under the trade names Nuprin and Advil, it is not recommended for use in treating children under 12 years of age without a doctor's supervision. However, it can be very effective in relieving menstrual cramps in teen-age girls. Also, one medical study recently showed that ibuprofen in combination with the antibiotic tetracycline may effectively combat acne. Tetracycline is often used to fight acne, but evidently, for some teen-agers, adding ibuprofen to the antibiotic may increase that drug's effectiveness. Although the reason for this is not fully known, some researchers believe the anti-inflammatory action of ibuprofen is responsible for the increased effectiveness. At any rate, some skin doctors are now considering using ibuprofen for teenagers who have not responded to tetracycline alone.

Side Effects

Although ibuprofen produces fewer side effects than aspirin, it can cause itching, rashes, stomach upset, and dizziness. Ibuprofen is less toxic in large doses than either aspirin or acetaminophen, but it may lead to kidney damage when taken in large doses over a prolonged period of time.

When Not to Use Ibuprofen

Ibuprofen should not be used by children under 12 unless supervised by a doctor. If your child is allergic or sensitive to aspirin, he or she should not use this medication. The same precautions about letting a fever run its course and about not dosing before a doctor's physical exam pertain here as well.

When to Use Ibuprofen

Ibuprofen can be used to reduce a fever and relieve minor pains as well as stiffness and aching.

How to Use Ibuprofen

Ibuprofen is available in 200 mg tablets. You can give your child one tablet every four to six hours as needed. If his or her symptoms do not respond to one tablet, you may give two tablets at the next dosage interval, but do not exceed six tablets in 24 hours. You should discuss this with your child's doctor, however. Have the child take the medication with food or milk to prevent stomach upset.

6

OVER-THE-COUNTER PRODUCTS

Most people are accustomed to treating their own and their children's minor ailments themselves, generally using medications and products they can buy without a doctor's prescription. These nonprescription items, also called *patent, over-the-counter,* or *OTC medicines,* are often an important part of a family's health care. Nevertheless, all medicines, whether prescription or OTC, have the potential to be dangerous. Buying and administering OTC medications wisely and safely, therefore, is an important responsibility of all parents.

HOW TO BUY

When buying medicines for your child, it is sometimes vital that you have access to professional information, especially on those occasions when you need advice about a specific OTC product. It is best, therefore, to select a store with a licensed pharmacist on duty. Of course, if you are simply picking up your usual brand of baby aspirin or some general medicine cabinet supplies, you are probably most interested in price or convenience, and a discount or grocery store is good enough. At those times when you want to purchase an OTC medication for your child's cough or skin rash and are unsure of what to buy, however, you should shop at a reputable drugstore or a drug department where there is a registered pharmacist on duty. While you cannot and should not count on a pharmacist to take the place of your physician, the pharmacist can give you helpful information about buying a patent remedy for treatment of a nonserious illness. Studies have shown that almost half of the consumers surveyed seek advice about minor health problems from their pharmacist at least once a year.

Select a drugstore that is convenient, one that you can make "your" drugstore. It may be a small, independent store, part of a large chain, or a drug department located in a discount department store or grocery. Government regulations and standards are the same for all pharmacies. Be certain to find out if the pharmacist is available at night and on weekends. (Although it really isn't true, it does seem that children most often get sick at night and on weekends.) You should be aware that in large drugstores you may not have a chance to get to know the pharmacist well because personnel are sometimes transferred or rotated from store to store. If such familiarity is important to you, it would be best to patronize an owner-operated pharmacy.

Several factors should be considered when choosing a pharmacy:

- Check out the pharmacy's hours. Does it provide after-hours emergency service?
- Does it have a delivery service that you can use if you are at home alone with a child too sick to go out?
- Is it convenient to your home?
- Does it carry a wide selection of products, including generic or private-label items that may be less expensive than well-known brand names?
- Are its prices competitive?
- Does it offer credit or accept major bank credit cards? (This latter point could be important if you expect to request deliveries or have a friend or neighbor pick up your order for you.)
- If it is part of a large chain, does your local store have computer capability that will enable it to forward your records to other stores in the chain?
- Is the pharmacist courteous, friendly, and, above all, helpful?

SELECTING THE PRODUCT

Before buying a specific product, you first have to determine exactly what it is you are treating. Is your child's nose stuffy? Does he or she have a fever? Does your teen-ager want an acne lotion? Once you have decided what symptom you are treating, choose a product that treats only that symptom. For example, if your child's nose is stuffy, use a decongestant, but not a decongestant combined with a pain reliever. Why give your child drugs that he or she does not need? Always try to select drugs that have a single action. If your child has a stuffy nose and a fever, buy two products; when the fever has disappeared or decreased, you can stop giving the drug for fever but continue the decongestant if needed. It's always a good idea to avoid unnecessary medications.

Talking to Your Pharmacist

If you do not know what kind of product to buy for your child's specific problem, or if you have selected what you consider to be an appropriate item but are unsure about your choice, ask your pharmacist for advice. Explain the illness or ailment to the pharmacist, and ask for a recommendation of an OTC product; then ask specifically about its safety and effectiveness. Find out if it will interact with any other drugs your child may be taking, either OTC or presription. Keep in mind that medicines that are given orally can react with other medicines that are used topically, that is, applied externally. If your child has allergies, be certain to mention that to the pharmacist; he or she will then know to suggest a medication that is least likely to trigger an allergic reaction.

Question your pharmacist about the best way to administer a particular medication to your child. Ask about anything on the product's label that is unclear. For instance, if the directions say to take the medicine every four hours, is it best to take it before or after meals, or doesn't it make any difference? Should the medication be taken throughout the night as well as during the waking hours? Find out if there are any side effects and, if so, what you can do about them. Be especially certain to learn which side effects are minor and which warrant the attention of your doctor. Finally, ask the pharmacist if the product you have selected is the most economical yet effective way to treat your child's ailment. Your pharmacist can help you save money by suggesting alternative products that may be cheaper or by vouching for the safety and effectiveness of a lower-priced generic or store-brand product. In general, this latter point applies only when you are treating an ailment yourself; if your physician recommends or prescribes a particular item by brand name, you should follow his or her advice.

Reading the Label

Before buying any product, read the label carefully. The label should include this information:

- the name and type of drug
- its purpose
- dosage (be sure the drug has dosage directions for children)
- the maximum safe dosage
- instructions for the drug's use
- directions for storing the drug
- warnings, including possible side effects, drug interactions, and special health problems that might interfere with the use of the drug
- the drug's active ingredients (manufacturers are not required to specify concentrations or strengths of ingredients for some products; if the concentrations are not listed, don't buy the product)
- expiration date (the date beyond which the drug should not be used for the sake of safety or effectiveness)
- the name and address of the manufacturer

If all of this information is not on the label, do not buy the drug. Even if your pharmacist is able to fill in the missing information for you, you may not remember it a month later if you have to use the medicine again. If the information is present but confusing, talk to the pharmacist and ask for clarification. Always be certain you know exactly what a drug will or will not do and how it should be used.

HOW TO USE OTC MEDICATIONS

Read the label and follow the directions. The importance of using an OTC medicine exactly the way the manufacturer suggests cannot be overemphasized. Extensive research and testing goes into health care products before they reach the market, and it is only reasonable to heed the advice of the firm that has formulated and tested the product.

Even after you have read the label in the drugstore and asked the druggist to clarify any unclear information, *read the label again* after you get home and before you administer the medication. It's a good idea, in fact, to reread the label each time you give a medicine to your child.

Remember, practically any substance, even very common and seemingly harmless products, can be harmful if given incorrectly. Just as with prescription medications, misuse of an OTC drug can render it at best ineffective and at worst dangerous.

Dosage

Giving your child an inaccurate dosage of an OTC drug is a common mistake. If you give the child too little, you are not doing any good. Obviously, if you give the child too much, you are risking an overdose. When dealing with medicines, it is definitely possible to have too much of a good thing. Never assume that if you give your child two doses instead of one he or she will get well twice as fast. By the same token, giving a dose every two hours instead of every four hours as recommended will not cause the symptoms to disappear sooner. On the contrary, such actions can cause an overdose that can be exceedingly dangerous. Always check the dosage recommendations on the label and strictly adhere to them.

Using proper measuring devices is important when giving accurate doses of medicines. Never use an ordinary teaspoon to measure liquid medications; their shapes and sizes vary, and you could risk giving your child too little or too much medicine.

How to Measure Your Child's Medications

Accuracy of dosage is critical to any drug's effectiveness. It is important to measure carefully every time you give your child medicines and to see that the full amount recommended is taken.

LIQUIDS

Instead of using an ordinary teaspoon or tablespoon when measuring your child's medicine, ask your pharmacist for a medication spoon. One of the most useful children's health care gadgets to come on the market, this kind of spoon is actually two utensils in one. It looks like a laboratory test tube with a spoon-shaped collar attached to it. The whole thing is molded of clear plastic, and the tube portion is marked off in teaspoon measures. You use it by pouring the liquid into the tube up to the desired mark, then inserting the spoon portion into your child's mouth and tipping the tube up to pour the medicine in. Children are used to the feel of a spoon in their mouths and will generally accept it readily. In addition to its accuracy, a medication spoon is much easier to use and less likely to spill when you are trying to give medicine to a squirming baby.

DROPS

If the medicine you are using is a liquid that is to be measured in drops, or if you are administering eye- or eardrops, ask your pharmacist to open the package and show you the dropper. If the dropper is not calibrated for accurate measuring, ask the druggist for one that is. If it is necessary to use a dropper other than the one that comes with the medication, wash it thoroughly after each

Text continues on next page

use and keep it in a plastic bag where you store the medicine itself. Don't trust your judgment to determine how much two or three drops is; use a clearly marked dropper.

TABLETS

Sometimes children have difficulty swallowing pills, and you may want to crush the tablets and put them into water, juice, milk, or food. (*Never* attempt to give any kind of tablet to an infant or to a coughing child. There is a strong likelihood of its lodging in the child's throat and blocking the airway.) Ask your pharmacist if you can crush tablets and put them into food or liquids. You must make sure, of course, that your child consumes the entire amount of medicine-containing food so that he or she also gets the full amount of medicine. For this reason you should mix the medicine with only a small amount of food or beverage. Some pills, because they are not intended to start working until they are in the stomach, have a protective coating that seals in the medicine and prevents it from dissolving until it actually reaches the stomach. Some medications are available in a variety of forms, and you may be able to purchase a liquid equivalent that will be more easily administered than a pill.

YOUR CHILD'S RESPONSE

When you have given a medication to a child, check his or her response to the drug. Does the product seem to be doing what it is supposed to do? Do you or your child notice any side effects? (Read the label again so that you know what to watch for.) Is your child behaving differently from usual? Is there no improvement at all?

If your child suddenly becomes very lethargic or very ill, call the poison control center immediately. Even a normal dose of an OTC product can act as an overdose if your child is allergic or is unable to tolerate one of the product's ingredients.

Always keep a close watch on your child when you are administering any drug, including OTC products, and instruct caregivers other than yourself to do the same and report any unusual behavior to you. Do not discard any patent medicines or their containers until you are sure your child has recovered from his or her ailment. If you have to call the doctor, you will want to be able to outline exactly how your child has reacted to the medication and also tell the doctor just what the medication contained.

CALLING THE DOCTOR

There will be times when self-treatment does not work. When you are treating your child with OTC products and observing his or her response, be prepared to call the doctor if there is no response at all, if the child's condition worsens, or if there is an adverse reaction. Also, call the doctor if you accidentally give the child too much medication.

When you call the doctor, be prepared to describe the illness in detail; be specific about degree of fever, cough, and so forth. Jot down notes before you call if you think you might forget a detail. Also, look up and write down the name and telephone number of your pharmacy in case your doctor decides a prescription is necessary. (As suggested in Chapter 3, you should already have the pharmacy's number taped to the bottom of your telephone along with those of the poison control center, doctor, hospital, and police and fire departments.)

Take the container of OTC medication with you to the telephone so that you can tell the doctor how you have treated the child. In addition to the name of the OTC drug, tell the doctor the dosage you have used, how often you gave the dosage, and how long you have been treating your child with the medication. Describe any side effects or any unusual behavior your child has displayed.

Have a pencil and paper at hand to write down any instructions or suggestions your doctor may give you. Don't be surprised if the physician suggests that you stop using the OTC preparation and simply let nature take its course. Sometimes time alone is the preferred treatment. The human body is extremely resilient and capable of healing itself.

It is important to remember that, despite the fact that they are considered safe enough to sell without a doctor's prescription, OTC products are still chemicals and can cause problems. They can also mask a serious illness by relieving symptoms that point to that illness. Suppose you give your child aspirin to relieve fever and then take the child to the doctor. The doctor will not be able to measure the fever or to note other symptoms, such as inflammation or pain, that the aspirin relieves. The point is, you should not use OTC products simply to relieve symptoms without trying to learn their underlying cause. Once you know what's wrong and are treating it, OTC products can help relieve minor symptoms and provide comfort while your child recovers. If you have any questions about OTC medication, consult your child's doctor, who knows your child and your family.

7

PRESCRIPTION DRUGS

How many times have you taken your child to your doctor for an illness and received a prescription as part of the treatment? Have you then done what most parents do, namely, accept the prescription without question, take it to the pharmacy, and administer the medication to your child according to the directions on the label? In most cases, there is nothing wrong with that, but remember, medicines are chemicals that you are putting into your child's body. These chemicals are supposed to be beneficial, of course, but every person reacts differently to a chemical. You should know as much as you can about what you are giving your child and why.

HOW CHILDREN REACT

It's important to understand that children, especially infants, are unusually sensitive to drugs. The ability of a child's body to use and eliminate drugs is not as fully developed as that of an adult. In babies, particularly, drugs enter the central nervous system, including the brain, more quickly and easily. Even a lotion or topical ointment applied to a baby's skin to treat a rash, for example, is absorbed more quickly and to a greater degree than in older children or adults. This may lead to a generalized effect throughout the body, although the topical medication is intended to have only a local effect on the rash.

The body of an older child is better able to handle the effects of a drug, but keep in mind that this ability still does not yet equal that of an adult. In addition, don't forget that, unlike adults, all children are growing; any drug should be evaluated for the possibility of impairing or changing normal growth and development. For instance, a drug that may be prescribed to treat hyperactivity (also called *hyperkinesis* or *attention deficit disorder*) in children may cause a slowdown in their growth. Doctors prescribing this drug, called methylphenidate (trade name Ritalin), may recommend permitting an occasional "drug holiday" for a specific period of time in order to allow the child under treatment to reestablish normal growth and development.

What all of this means is that you should realize what kind of responsibility you have when you are administering medications to your child. Once you have left the doctor's office and the pharmacy, you and you alone are responsible for how that medication is used. You should understand how the drug works; what to expect in the way of side effects, if any; what side effects or reactions are minor and expected and which ones warrant a prompt call to your doctor.

The doctor and the pharmacist are professionally trained to know about drugs, but you as a parent also become part of the medical team when you are expected to administer medication. In that case, shouldn't you tap into the professional expertise of your doctor and pharmacist before you begin administering medication to your child?

THE FIRST STEP

The first step in using a prescription occurs in your doctor's office when you are handed the prescription. This is the time to ask specific questions about the drug(s) so that you are certain about (1) what you are supposed to do and (2) what the drug is supposed to do. Ask about side effects and warning signs. Ask how your child should respond to this drug. Ask how to give the drug. Ask about its cost. This is

What to Ask the Doctor

Sometimes when you take your child to see the doctor, particularly at those times when you have had to be squeezed into the doctor's schedule on an emergency basis, he or she may not have much time to spend with you. Nevertheless, there are still questions to which you need answers regarding prescribed medications. You can save your time and the doctor's—and still get all the information you need—if you jot down these questions ahead of time and run through them quickly when you see your doctor.

- What is the medication's name—both brand name and generic name? (The generic name is usually the name of the ingredients.)
- What is the drug supposed to do?
- How should I give the medication?
- How much medicine should I give at each dose?
- How often should I give this medicine?
- Am I supposed to give this medicine on a regular schedule—such as every four hours—or should I give it as my child needs it? How will I know when or if he or she needs it?
- If I am supposed to give this medicine every four hours, does that mean throughout the night or only during my child's waking hours?
- Should I give this medicine with food, milk, or juice, or on an empty stomach? Should I make sure my child drinks more water than usual?
- Are there any foods or beverages my child should or should not consume while taking this drug?
- Will this drug interfere with any lab tests my child may have?
- Are there minor side effects that I should expect, and can I take care of them myself?

Text continues on next page

- Are there any adverse side effects that I should call you about?
- Will this drug interact with any other medicines, including over-the-counter remedies, that my child is taking?
- If my child has allergies, could he or she be allergic to this drug?
- What should I do if I miss a dose?
- If my child refuses to take this medication in the form it comes in, can I crush or break a tablet, open a capsule, or pour a liquid into a small amount of food?
- If this drug is to be given for a prolonged period of time, will it have any effect on my child's growth?
- Finally, what is perhaps the most important question of all: Is this drug really necessary? Do the benefits outweigh any risks?

the time to clarify any doubts or questions you may have. One of the best ways to do so is to use the following list of questions as a checklist when you discuss a prescription drug with your child's doctor.

Let's take a closer look at some of these questions. It is important that you know the name of the medicine your child is taking in case he or she experiences a reaction to it and you have to tell someone other than your doctor what it is. Also, you might ask your doctor to indicate on the prescription form that the pharmacist is to fill the prescription with the least expensive compound. Keep in mind that some medicines your doctor prescribes may have generic or even OTC equivalents that cost less than a brand name product.

When you ask the doctor precisely what the drug is supposed to do, also find out if the prescribed medicine will simply speed up the desired healing process or if it is essential to the cure itself. In other words, is there a likelihood that your child may get over the present problem with no medicine at all, although it may take a day or two longer?

As you prepare to give the drug, are the instructions clear? For example, is the instruction "Give four times a day" the same as "Give every six hours"? In general, these two sets of instructions are not interchangeable. If the label tells you to give the medicine four times a day, that means you should give the four doses of medication at evenly spaced intervals throughout the waking hours. However, "every six hours" means that you must be very precise and give the medicine every six hours around the clock. In this case, of course, you will have to wake the child.

The reason for differing timing instructions is that different medications require different periods of time to become effective. Some medications must be given at precisely spaced intervals around the clock in order to provide constant benefits. Others can be effective if given only during the day when the child is awake. Be sure you understand when and how often a drug is to be administered.

FOLLOWING THE DIRECTIONS

It is important to know exactly how long you should continue administering any medicine. Should it be for a certain number of days or just until your child seems well again? Some medicines have both symptomatic relief properties and specific disease-curing functions. Your child could feel better and appear well in a couple of days, and your doctor could still want you to continue giving the medicine. In cases of strep throat, for example, it is necessary to continue the medication for at least 10 days in order to cure the condition, even though your child may appear perfectly well after only three or four days. Stopping the medication too soon can cause a relapse or complications. Quite often, the symptoms disappear long before the healing process is completed. Therefore, if your prescription label instructs you to "give until finished," "give for 10 full days," or "continue for two weeks," carry out this instruction to the letter. This type of medication has a bigger job than just relieving symptoms.

Also ask your doctor about giving the medication with or without food. Find out as well if your child should avoid certain foods or drinks while taking this drug. For example, some of the tetracycline antibiotics should not be taken with food, especially dairy products; dairy products interfere with the body's absorption of the medicine. On the other hand, sometimes foods can be beneficial when eaten with a medication. Yogurt, for instance, can help prevent the mild diarrhea that may be a side effect of some antibiotics. When an antibiotic is given to kill bacteria causing, say, an earache, the drug kills other bacteria in the body as well. Some bacteria normally living in the intestines are beneficial, and if the medication kills them, diarrhea may be the result. Yogurt that has been cultured with beneficial bacteria may help restore the normal balance of the intestine and thus prevent the diarrhea.

Some medicines are to be given on an "as needed" basis. But what does "as needed" mean? What should you look for before applying an ointment or cream? How will you know when your child needs another tablet? Get specific instructions so that you can keep your child comfortable and avoid overdosing.

Some medications, such as drugs for urinary tract infections, require the flushing effect of more than the usual amount of water passing through the kidneys. It is very important that you know whether the prescription your doctor writes involves such a medicine.

Check out each of these points with your doctor before giving your child any medicine the doctor prescribes. It is just possible he or she may forget to inform you completely. Sometimes a physician may rely on a pharmacist to inform a patient fully, and the pharmacist may assume the physician has already done so. *Make it your responsibility to find out.*

If the doctor is going to perform any blood, urine, or other kinds of tests, ask whether the prescribed medicine will have any effect on their results. It may be best to wait until after the tests before beginning to administer the medicine.

YOUR CHILD'S RESPONSE

You will probably notice some change in your child's condition once you have begun giving him or her medication. Ideally, it will be a diminishment in the illness for which the medicine was prescribed. But some adverse reactions could also occur. Is it a normal side effect of the drug, for example, for your child to become sleepy or complain of a slightly dry throat or upset stomach? Are there more serious reactions you should be watching for, such as a tendency to bleed more than usual from a slight cut or blurry vision? Which side effects are transitory and expected, and which ones should alarm you? Some drugs are very powerful chemicals; know what you are dealing with.

Some allergies seem to occur in groups. That is, when a child is allergic to one substance, it may be assumed that he or she will also be allergic to another. In general, your physician will not know what your child's allergies are unless you describe them; do not fail to do so before accepting any medicine prescription. And be certain to tell your doctor if you are treating your child with any over-the-counter remedies. Keep in mind that many medicines are compounds of more than one substance. While your child may not have a reaction to the primary drug, he or she may be allergic to one of the other drugs contained in the compound. It is even possible to have a reaction to the substance used to coat a pill while having no reaction to the actual medicine the pill contains.

So often when a child is sick, he or she is also fussy. At such times it may be difficult to get the child to take his or her medicine. Rather than add to your child's discomfort and your own frustration, ask the doctor if there is a pleasant and easy way to give the medicine. Is there a liquid form, for instance, that would be easier to swallow than a pill, or is there a way to disguise the taste that your child objects to? Can a pill be crushed or a capsule opened to be mixed with a bit of your child's favorite food?

YOUR RESPONSIBILITY

Just as your doctor has the duty to answer your questions, you have an equally important responsibility: you must tell the doctor everything that pertains to your child's health:

- Is your child being seen and treated by another doctor?
- Is your child taking other prescription drugs?
- Does your child use OTC medicines on a regular basis?
- Is your child allergic to anything?
- Is your child on a special diet or taking vitamin and mineral supplements?

Your doctor needs to know this information so that he or she can prescribe safely and effectively. Don't hesitate to remind your doctor also of any drug or treatment he or she may have recommended; if your doctor is not reading your child's record at the moment the prescription is being written, he or she may not remember that you were told to give your child vitamins with fluoride supplements. Be forthright and frank about all of your child's health practices. Most especially, tell your doctor about any other doctor who is treating your child and any other drugs your child is taking. Incidentally, the converse is true: be certain to inform any other doctors, dentists, or medical specialists of what your child is taking and what medical professionals are treating your child.

READING THE PRESCRIPTION

Many people regard doctors' prescriptions as one of the great mysteries of life. Actually, they aren't terribly difficult to understand once you learn what various abbreviations mean. Prescriptions are written in a kind of shorthand that is based on Latin and Greek terms, a carryover from the days when formal education included study of those languages. Nowadays it is unlikely that most physicians or pharmacists could even tell you the precise foreign-language meanings of the abbreviations they use, but they continue to use them nonetheless. Chalk it up to the mystique of the medical professions, but don't let it intimidate you.

When you are handed a prescription form by your child's doctor, read it over. If there are any terms you are unable to understand, ask for an explanation. And don't be satisfied with a reassuring "Don't worry about it. It's what your child needs. The drugstore will give you directions." Tell your doctor you want to know what the medicine is and you want to know exactly how to use it. Later on you can ask the pharmacist the same questions. You can't know too much when you are dealing with your child's health.

When you do have the prescription filled, it will not be possible for you to know whether the pharmacist has carried out your doctor's orders properly unless you can knowledgeably compare the medicine's label with what was written on the prescription form. Mistakes can happen; even something so simple as a typographical error can occur when the pharmacist types out the instruction label. Pay attention to what your physician and pharmacist tell you and don't hesitate to ask questions any time you fail to understand precisely what you, as your child's caregiver, are supposed to do and to watch for.

BUYING THE PRESCRIBED DRUG

When you buy a prescription medication, talk to your pharmacist. You'll want to discuss any new or additional questions that you may have neglected to ask your physician. The pharmacist can also inform you about price and money-saving ideas. Although he or she may not know the treatment regimen your doctor has decided upon, the pharmacist does know about drugs and can tell you about the product you are buying.

It is also a good idea to buy all of your drugs from the same pharmacy. A good professional pharmacy maintains detailed records for each customer, and often the pharmacist is the first person to discover that a new prescription will interact with a drug the patient is already using. Even though you think you have told your doctor about any other drugs your child is taking, you may have forgotten one, especially a home remedy or a nonprescription medicine. In addition, a pharmacist who is familiar with your records and your family will know how to suggest OTC products that will not interfere with any prescription drugs you are taking. It is important to develop a good working relationship with a professional pharmacist.

Pharmaceutical Abbreviations

Abbreviation	Meaning	Latin (unless otherwise indicated)
a; aa	each	ana (Greek)
a c	before meals	ante cibum
ad lib	as wanted	ad libitum
aq	water	aqua
bib	drink	bibe
bid	twice a day	bis in die
bin	twice a night	bis in noctus
C	centrigrade	Centrigradus
c	with	cum
cap(s)	capsule(s)	capsula
cc	cubic centimeter	(French)
cg	centigram	(French)
cm	centimeter	(French)
comp	compound	compositus
dil	dilute	dilue
dr	dram(s)	drachma
elix	elixir	(Arabic)
et	and	et
ext	extract	extractum
F	Fahrenheit	(proper name)
Fld	fluid	fluidus
ft	make (let there be made)	fiat
gm	gram	gramme (French)
gn	grain	granum
gtt	drops	guttae
H	hour	hora
h n	tonight	hac nocte
h s	at bedtime	hora somni
hypo	hypodermically	(Greek)
i; ii; iii	one; two; three	(Roman numerals)
L	liter	litra
liq	liquid; fluid	liquor
mg	milligram	(French)

Text continues on next page

mist	mixture	mistura
ml	milliliter	(French)
no	number	numero
non rep	don't repeat (refill)	non repetatur
noxt	at night	nocte, noxte
os	mouth	os, ora
oz	ounce	uncia
p c	after meals	post cibum
per	by, through	per
pil(s)	pill(s)	pilula
p o	by mouth	per os
prn	as needed	pro re nata
pulv	powder	pulvis
qh	every hour	quaque hora
q2h	every two hours	——
q4h	every four hours	——
qid	four times a day	quater in die
q s	sufficient quantity	quantum sufficiat
quotid	every day	quotidie
q v	as much as desired	quantum vis
Rx	take	recipe
rep	repeat (refill)	repetatur
S	mark	signa
s	without	sine
Sig	label (directions)	signetur
sol	solution	solutio
solv	dissolve	solve
ss	half	semis
stat	immediately	statim
syr	syrup	syrups
T	temperature	temperatura
tab(s)	tablet(s)	tabella
tid	three times a day	ter in die
tin	three times a night	ter in nocte
tr; tinct	tincture	tinctura
ung	ointment	unguentum

Note: Any of these abbreviations may appear with or without periods. If your child's doctor uses abbreviations other than those above, ask what they mean.

What to Ask the Pharmacist

- What is the maximum amount of this medication that my child should have in one day?
- How should this drug be stored?
- What is the expiration date for this medication? How long will it be safe and effective?
- Is there an OTC product that is equally effective and perhaps less expensive?
- Is there a generic equivalent that is just as effective and cheaper?
- How many refills will be available?
- In your experience, what are the common side effects of this drug? When should I call my doctor about a side effect?
- What have you found to be the best way to give this drug to a child?
- Can I mix the drug with food by crushing or breaking a tablet, opening a capsule, or pouring in a liquid?
- How much of this medication should I buy at one time? (This question applies to a medication for a long-term condition; for an acute illness the doctor generally prescribes a limited amount of medication to handle the short-term condition.)
- Will this medication interact with any other prescription drugs or OTC medicines that my child is taking?
- Is there anything else I should know about this medication?
- Is there a printed patient education brochure available for this medication, and if so, may I have a copy?

You will note that the questions you should ask your pharmacist may often be the same ones you have asked your doctor. This is because the doctor and the pharmacist are approaching your child's illness from two different angles: the doctor is the expert on illness and treatment, and the pharmacist is the expert on the chemical makeup of medications. While your doctor and your pharmacist may give you much the same answers to your questions, the pharmacist might give you a little more information about the practical administration of drugs. It also doesn't hurt to ask the same question twice so that you are absolutely certain that you know what to do. By the way, if your child begins to exhibit an adverse reaction to a prescription medication, phone your physician at once; don't call the pharmacist. Don't rely on your pharmacist for treatment; that's the job of your doctor.

STORAGE

Your pharmacist can give you detailed information about storing your drugs. In general, most prescription drugs can be stored at room temperature but not in a direct sunlight or near heat or moisture. When a medication requires special storage conditions, the pharmacist generally includes that information on the label. Nevertheless, to be on the safe side, ask the pharmacist about proper storage.

If a medicine's label says it is to be refrigerated, that does not mean you should store it in the freezer. Frozen medications often break down and lose their effectiveness when

---

Medication Storage Temperatures

Room temperature: generally 59–86°F (15–30°C)
Cool: generally 46–59°F (8–15°C)
Refrigerated: generally 36–46°F (2–8°C)
Cold: below 46°F (8°C)
Excessive heat: above 104°F (40°C)

Note: Regardless of the specified storage temperature, you should always make sure all medicine containers are tightly sealed to prevent moisture from entering. Store all medicines away from light whenever possible.

thawed. Ask the pharmacist about the proper storage temperature.

Ironically, one of the worst places to store medication is the bathroom medicine cabinet. Heat and humidity in the average bathroom can change the medication's composition. Furthermore, the bathroom medicine cabinet is easily accessible to curious children. The best place to store medications that do not require refrigeration is a locked box or chest in a cool, dark spot; take care not to allow your child to gain access to the key. If you cannot keep your medicines in a locked chest, at least store them on a high shelf that is inaccessible to climbing children.

SAVING MONEY

Naturally, as with any other purchase you make for your family, you want the prescription drugs you buy to be as inexpensive as possible yet still safe and effective. Remember, however, that the key words are *safe* and *effective*. That is the most important consideration when you administer drugs to your child.

OTC Substitutes

Sometimes you can substitute a less expensive over-the-counter medicine for a prescription. Of course, this should be done only with the approval of your doctor. You should also discuss it with your pharmacist. For example, currently ibuprofen, a painkiller, is available both as a prescription drug and over the counter. The OTC brands were less expensive when they first entered the market. Then the manufacturers of the prescription versions lowered their prices to meet the competition. The OTC products contain only 200 mg of medication, however, while the prescription drugs come in dosages of 400–600 mg; you may have to take more of the OTC drug to achieve the desired effect. Thus, in this case the OTC may not be cheaper. It is always wise to check out the possibility of making substitutions with your pharmacist and your doctor.

Generic Drugs

Another way that you may be able to save money when buying prescription drugs is to investigate generic drugs. A generic drug is not protected by trademark registration. Thus a generic drug does not carry a brand name; often its name is simply the name of its ingredient or a shortened version thereof.

A generic drug is often less expensive than a brand name drug because it is not advertised as much. Ask your doctor to specify a generic drug on the prescription. Many states permit the pharmacist to fill a prescription with the least expensive equivalent, but in those areas where this is not allowed, the doctor can specify a generic substitute on the prescription.

It is important to remember that substituting a generic drug for a brand name drug is not always possible or advisable. Some drugs are not available generically. Furthermore, some generic drugs are not noticeably less expensive than their trade name counterparts. The most significant consideration, of course, is safety and effectiveness. Although the United States Food and Drug Administration (FDA), which regulates the pharmaceutical industry, claims that there is little or no evidence that there are differences between trade name and generic drugs, some differences have surfaced between generics and certain brands. This may be of no consequence if the difference is small or irrelevant. For example, if a generic does not begin working as quickly as its brand name counterpart, this may not be important in a minor illness. If, however, the drug is being used to open air passages during an acute allergic reaction when time can mean life or death, you want the drug that acts most quickly. If you have questions, ask your doctor.

In general, however, generic drugs are less expensive and as safe and effective as brand name drugs. In fact, the reputation of generic drugs has improved in recent years, and as of 1984 there is legislation that will allow many more generic equivalents to be manufactured and marketed. Using generics is a good way to save money when you buy prescription drugs.

Quantity Buying

Just as buying the large, economy size of laundry detergent saves money, so occasionally does buying large quantities of medication. This, of course, applies only to medications for long-term or chronic conditions. Most of the medications prescribed for children are for short-term, acute illnesses, such as respiratory infections or ear infections. However, if your child is taking medication on long-term basis, ask your doctor about prescribing a larger amount per prescription so that you can take advantage of the savings. Remember, too, that the shelf life and expiration date of the medication may indicate how much extra medication you can buy or whether you can do so. You may also decide that having large quantities of a medication in a house where young children live is not a particularly good idea unless you have a foolproof and secure storage system.

8

GIVING MEDICATIONS

Administering medications to your child is an important responsibility. By being responsible for giving medicine to your child, you join your doctor and pharmacist as a member of the health team caring for your child.

When you are about to give your child medication, assume from the beginning that he or she will take it without objection. If you seem hesitant or uncertain, your child may reflect that uncertainty. You should never use force to try to coerce your child to take medicine; neither should you allow him or her to refuse to take it. A calm matter-of-fact approach is best. Let your child know that his or her treatment is a cooperative effort, but be firm about the fact that taking the medicine is a requirement and not an issue for debate or bargain. Even though your child may be fussy and feeling bad, don't allow that to become an excuse for skipping part of the treatment. By omitting an uncomfortable treatment, you not only are not helping your child get well; you are also setting a potentially dangerous precedent for your future manipulation by the child.

Along the same lines, it is unwise and downright hazardous to attempt to bribe a child to take medicine by claiming that the medicine is candy. Many medications are flavored and sweetened, so a child might believe that they *are* candy. You are risking the child's taking the medicine behind your back and perhaps getting an overdose.

Obviously, giving the correct amount of medicine at the

correct time should be your main goal. After all, you want your child to get well again as soon as possible. However, there are appropriate ways of administering each kind of medication so that the child receives just the right dosage. Knowing how to administer medication will ensure that the medicine is being used properly, that your child is getting the full benefit of the drug, and that you are not inadvertently giving a potentially toxic dose of a substance that would otherwise be beneficial. Furthermore, your child is more likely to cooperate if you are deft and smooth when giving medications.

LIQUIDS

Before using a liquid medication, check the label to see if you should shake the bottle. If you are to shake the container, be certain always to shake it thoroughly. If the solution separates out into separate ingredients, you run the risk of at best an ineffective dose of the medicine's active ingredient and at worst a toxic dose of concentrated medication. Open the bottle carefully, holding the top away from your body and unscrewing the cap slowly; some medications build up froth and pressure when shaken and burst out when the container is opened.

Internal Use

If the liquid is to be taken internally, be certain to measure the dose accurately. Your kitchen teaspoon won't do; ask your pharmacist for a special medication spoon. If your child won't take medication from anything except his or her own spoon, measure the dose in the medication spoon before pouring it into the child's spoon.

For very young or very ill children some parents find that using a medicine dropper or even a syringe works best. You can first measure the dose in the properly calibrated spoon and then place it in the syringe or dropper. Insert the dropper or syringe into the child's mouth in the cheek, and then gently and slowly release the medication. Do not squirt the liquid directly toward the back of the throat; the child is liable to choke.

External Use

If the liquid medication is to be applied topically (externally) to the skin, follow the instructions carefully. Do not pour the medication into your cupped hand; you may spill it or waste more than you need to. Instead, pour it on a small piece of cotton or gauze and apply it gently to the affected area. Rub it in with your finger or with the gauze. Don't use such a large piece of gauze that most of the medication is absorbed into the applicator. For small areas, you might want to use a cotton-tipped applicator to apply the medication. Never put the applicator or gauze directly into the container; you may contaminate the contents. Hold the bottle over the sink or a container to catch any spillage and pour a little liquid onto the applicator. After each application, discard the applicator. Select a new one each time you administer another dose.

TABLETS AND CAPSULES

Most medications prescribed for children, especially young children, are available in liquid or chewable forms. However, if you are using the tablet or capsule form of a drug, there are ways of administering the medicine to a child easily.

The first rule of thumb is not to have a child under five years of age try to swallow a whole tablet or capsule. No matter how "grown up" they seem, their throat passageways are still very small. A young child can easily choke on or inhale a pill or capsule. The best way to give the medication is to crush it and stir it into a small amount of applesauce, juice, or ice cream. It is essential that the amount of food be very small, because the child must eat all the food or drink all the juice in order to receive the full dose of medicine. Often a sick child has a sore throat or little or no appetite and will refuse to eat more than one or two spoonfuls of food. The easiest way to crush a tablet is to place it in the bowl of a soup spoon and crush it with the back of the bowl of another soup spoon.

Before doing this, however, be sure to ask your doctor if

the medication you're giving can be crushed or if a capsule can be opened. Some medications must be swallowed whole in order to be effective. Although most doctors would not prescribe such a medication for a child, and over-the-counter products for children are usually crushable, it never hurts to double-check before giving the medicine in this manner.

An older child may be able to swallow pills and capsules. Tell your child to wet or rinse his or her mouth and then place the tablet or capsule on the back of the tongue, take a sip of water, and swallow. Be certain that the child has a full glass of water in his or her hand before placing the pill in the mouth; many children need several sips of water to get a pill down. It is also a good idea to have the child finish the entire glass of water. If your child has trouble taking a tablet or capsule, you might ask your pharmacist about a special cup or glass that automatically pops the pill into the child's mouth with the first swallow of water.

However he or she takes a pill, be certain to stay with your child and watch for signs of choking. Never leave a child alone while he or she is swallowing a tablet or capsule. One way you can help your child gain practice in swallowing pills and capsules smoothly without choking or gagging is to take advantage of those occasions when a child needs an over-the-counter remedy for a minor ailment—an aspirin to ease the pain of a muscle strain, for example. Encourage the child to swallow rather than chew the tablet. Never experiment with "pills" by using candies such as M&Ms, however. You should not associate medicines with candy; drugs mistaken for candy by a child can be lethal. It's a good idea as well to remove any bottles of candy "pills" from play doctor and nurse kits before giving them to a child.

CREAMS AND OINTMENTS

Creams and ointments are most often designed to treat what are called *local ailments* on the skin. That is, the condition affects only the area where it is located. Therefore, most creams and ointments will most often affect only the area on which they are applied. However, you must remember that in very young children, especially infants, topical medication can be absorbed more readily than in older children and adults and can have systemwide effects. Therefore, you should exercise care when applying any creams or ointments to babies or very young children.

It is best to apply a thin layer of an ointment or cream; too thick a layer can provide too high a dose of the medication, besides wasting money.

Before applying one of these medications, moisten the affected area of skin with clean, warm water and blot dry. Administer the medication according to the directions on the label and massage it into the skin until it disappears. An ointment will leave a greasy feeling on the skin, whereas a cream should disappear completely into the skin. If you have a choice of using an ointment or a cream, bear in mind that a cream will not leave a greasy feeling, nor will it stain clothing. Creams are especially useful on hairy areas. On the other hand, an ointment will keep the skin soft and is particularly helpful if your child's skin is dry or chapped.

Some treatments with creams or ointments involve applying a wrap over the area, usually plastic kitchen film. If your child is under five years old, be careful when using such a wrap. It's best to use several small pieces of plastic rather than one continuous length because your child might unwrap the area and injure him- or herself with the plastic. The clinging nature of plastic film can cause suffocation if it is placed over a child's face, or it can cut off circulation if pulled into a ropelike shape and looped tightly around an arm or a leg. Also, if you hold the wrap in place with tape in order to avoid the possibility of impairing circulation, you should use several short pieces of tape rather than one long piece that extends all the way around an arm or leg.

If your doctor prescribes such a measure, ask for detailed instructions. Be certain to follow all of them, including the length of time the wrap is to be left on the skin. The purpose of a wrap is to hold the medication against the skin and to keep the skin moist for better absorption of the medicine. If a wrap is left on too long, however, too much medication may be absorbed. Never use a wrap without your doctor's approval.

EYEDROPS AND EYE OINTMENTS

The first step in administering medications into the eyes is to read the label and be certain that the medicine is indicated for use in the eyes. Some medications are formulated in different ways, depending on their purpose or use; just because a liquid and an ointment have the same name, you should not assume that their methods of application are the same. Also, check to make sure that the solution has not changed color and that the expiration date is still acceptable.

Wash your hands. Have your child sit or lie down. Gently pull down the lower eyelid to form a pouch. Hold the eyedropper close to the eye without touching it. Place the prescribed number of drops in the pouch. Do not place the medication directly on the eyeball; this may cause the child to blink and lose the medication. As you apply the drops, place a finger alongside the nose at the corner of the eye. This closes off a duct that may drain the drops out of the eye through the nose. Ask the child to close his or her eyes for a few minutes. Replace the dropper in the bottle without wiping it or otherwise touching it. Close the container tightly.

If you are using an ointment, squeeze the prescribed line of ointment into the pouch and tell the child to close his or her eyes and roll them around to spread the ointment across the surface of the eyeball. Do not allow the child to rub his or her eyes. When done according to directions, applying eye medications should be painless.

EARDROPS

As with any medication you are giving your child, be certain that the expiration date is acceptable and that the medication is intended to be used for the ears.

Before administering, you can warm eardrops by rolling the container back and forth between your hands. Never place the container in boiling water; the medication can become so hot that it may harm the ear canal. Furthermore, the heat may affect the medication's effectiveness.

To apply eardrops, have the child lie down or put his or her head down on a table with the ear to be treated tilted upward. Pull the child's earlobe downward and back. The drops should fill the canal. Place the prescribed number of drops in the ear canal, but do not allow the dropper to touch any part of the ear or ear canal. If the dropper touches an infected area, it will then contaminate the rest of the solution in the container. In that case, discard the contaminated bottle and get a new one. Continue to hold the earlobe and keep the ear tilted upward for about 10 seconds. Gently insert a small piece of clean cotton to prevent the drops from escaping from the ear. Replace the dropper in the container without cleaning or wiping it.

NOSE DROPS

Before giving nose drops, ask your child to blow his or her nose gently. If a child is unable to blow his or her nose, you might want to clean the nose out with cotton swabs.

Have your child lie down or tilt his or her head backward. Fill the dropper and place the prescribed number of drops in the nose. Keep the child's head tilted backward for about 10 seconds and then have the child either sniff gently two or three times or sit up and bend the head forward and downward. Take care that you do not touch the dropper to the nasal membranes; otherwise you may contaminate the contents of your container when you replace the dropper.

If your doctor has suggested a nasal spray, do not have the child tilt his or her head backward. Instead, simply insert the sprayer into the nose without touching the nasal membranes. Ask the child to sniff gently while you squeeze the container. Do not release your grip on the sprayer until you have removed it from the nose so that bacteria and other contaminants cannot be drawn into the sprayer. Have the child sniff two or three times.

Unless otherwise directed by your doctor, you should not use a nasal spray or nose drops for more than three days in a row. Nose drops and sprays tend to have what is known as a *rebound effect*. Nose drops and sprays work to decrease nasal congestion by constricting blood vessels in the nose. After about three days, this activity backfires because the constant constricting of the vessels tires the vessels and causes them to relax completely. The result is even more congestion.

On the other hand, if your doctor has prescribed drops or spray for a longer period of time, do not use one container for more than one week at a time. Buy a new container. Also, do not use the same container for more than one person. Each person in a household should have his or her own container of nose drops or nasal spray.

AEROSOL SPRAYS

As a general rule, aerosol packages are more expensive than nonaerosol forms such as creams and ointments. However, sometimes an aerosol spray is handy if the affected area is very tender to the touch or is very hairy.

To use an aerosol product, first read the directions and then shake the can. Hold the can upright four to six inches from the skin and press the nozzle. To avoid applying too heavily, use a series of short bursts, checking the coating after each one, rather than one long spray. Again, as with creams and ointments, take care not to apply too much.

You should never use the aerosol can around the eyes, nose, or mouth. In fact, avoid using it around the face altogether. The aerosol propellant gas can get into the eyes or be inhaled into the lungs, both of which can be painful or dangerous. If you must use the product on or near the face, spray it on your hand first and then apply it to the area you want to treat. If you are using this product only on the face, you will probably be better off choosing a cream or an ointment. Also be careful not to leave an aerosol can within the reach of your young child. It is an enticing object to play with, and the child could inadvertently spray the contents into his or her eyes.

Never use an aerosol product around a source of heat—an open flame, an electric heater, a nearby light bulb, or a lighted cigarette. Some aerosol cans use highly flammable propellant gases that can flash into flame.

MISSING A DOSE

Inevitably, you will miss giving a dose of medicine to your child at some time. What should you do in such a situation?

Each medication is unique; thus, there can be no general rule of thumb. One of your questions to your doctor when the medicine is prescribed should be "What if I miss a dose?" Be certain you understand how to handle this situation. This is one of those instructions you may want to write down. If you do not ask your doctor ahead of time and you do forget to give a dose, call your doctor. Under no circumstances should you automatically double the next dose; you could then give an overdose. Similarly, do not assume that if you give double doses of medicine your child will recover twice as fast. This is dangerous thinking.

A FINAL WORD

Remember, administering medicine to a child is an important responsibility. Reread these suggestions carefully from time to time so that you can fulfill your responsibility safely and smoothly. You'll find that your deft, self-assured, and matter-of-fact approach will work best with your child.

9

MANAGING
SIDE EFFECTS

Drugs are prescribed because of their beneficial or therapeutic effects on symptoms or illnesses. Each drug has what is called in medical language its own *indications*. An indication is a use for the drug that has been approved by the FDA. In other words, through testing and experimentation, research has found that a certain drug is indicated or suggested as an effective treatment for a certain condition.

Nevertheless, just as drugs offer desirable effects or benefits, they can also cause other responses that are unrelated to the illness being treated. These are called *side effects*.

Most side effects are a result of a drug's chemical activity and therefore are unavoidable. Many are undesirable, but most of them cause only minor inconvenience. Occasionally, however, a side effect becomes a serious condition or even a hazard in and of itself. These kinds of effects are often called *adverse reactions* to distinguish them from the more normal, expected, but unintended chemical activity of the drug while it works in the body. An adverse reaction is more serious than a side effect and may even become life-threatening. In fact, in some cases the risk from an adverse reaction to a drug far outweighs the benefit the drug offers.

How do you know what is a side effect and what is dangerous to your child?

LEARNING ABOUT SIDE EFFECTS

Whenever you receive a prescription or an OTC recommendation from your doctor or health care provider, you should be prepared to ask questions about the medication and its use. These questions should include "Should I expect side effects from this medicine? If so, what is normal and predictable, and what warrants medical attention? What is dangerous and needs emergency attention?"

No matter how these questions are answered in your doctor's office, the time may come when you will wonder at home what you should do if your child does not seem to respond to a drug or seems to show signs of a side effect. You will wonder if your child is displaying signs of a side effect or has developed additional symptoms of the illness. You may consult your notes and instructions from the doctor but still be uncertain about whether your child is displaying the typical symptoms of a normal expected side effect or if you should be concerned enough to call the doctor.

To be on the safe side, you should always call your doctor if you are concerned or confused. Sometimes even a minor side effect can be minimized or eliminated by a change in dosage or by something as simple as giving the drug with meals. If this is not possible, your doctor may be able to offer suggestions for managing the side effect. For example, some antibiotics can cause diarrhea as an expected side effect. This occurs because the antibiotic is designed to kill harmful bacteria, and in doing its job it also kills beneficial bacteria in the intestine. When the balance of bacteria in the intestine is disturbed, diarrhea can occur. However, if you give your child yogurt, the diarrhea will disappear because the fermented culture in the yogurt restores beneficial bacteria to the intestine.

If a side effect cannot be minimized or eliminated, your doctor may be able to give you some tips on how to help your child cope with the side effect. The accompanying chart will also offer some ideas on managing side effects.

Coping with Drug Side Effects

Side Effect	What to Do
Blurred vision	Call your doctor.
Breathing difficulty	Call your doctor.
Constipation	Increase fluid intake; call your doctor if constipation lasts more than two days; do not give laxative without asking doctor.
Diarrhea	Increase fluid intake; feed yogurt if child is taking antibiotic; call your doctor if diarrhea lasts more than three days.
Dizziness	Avoid hazardous activities; have child lie down with feet elevated; call your doctor if dizziness lasts more than two hours.
Drowsiness	Avoid games or activities requiring alertness; let child nap; call your doctor if child is difficult to rouse.
Dry mouth	Give child candy, chewing gum, or ice chips.
Dry nose, throat	Use a vaporizer; saltwater gargle.
Fever	Call your doctor if fever is new symptom.
Headache	Call your doctor.
Itching, skin rash	Call your doctor.
Nasal congestion	Ask your doctor if it is all right to use nose drops.
Stomach upset	Ask your doctor if it is all right to give medicine with food.

Guidelines for Calling the Doctor

Many side effects are self-limiting; that is, they disappear of their own accord without treatment. Others, however, require some management, and still others are warning signs that you should bring to the attention of your doctor. The following guidelines should help you decide which category a side effect falls into.

- Some drugs can cause dizziness. If this happens to your child, have the child lie down with his or her legs higher than the head. Sometimes dizziness can be handled by having the child sit with the head between the knees. Don't forget to prevent the child from engaging in any kind of hazardous activity requiring alertness and balance while the dizziness lasts. If dizziness becomes very pronounced or persists for more than two hours, call your doctor.

- Occasionally, a drug will cause a ringing, buzzing, or hollowness in the ears. This may be a symptom of aspirin overdose. It may also be a symptom of an ear infection. If the ringing persists beyond a day or if the child complains of any other ear problems call your doctor.

- Always call your doctor if your child has any trouble breathing or difficulty with vision or the eyes.

- Probably the most common side effects occur in the gastrointestinal system. This system consists of the mouth, esophagus, stomach, and small and large intestines. Many drugs can cause diarrhea, constipation, stomach upset, or dry mouth. Most of these side effects are self-limiting. As the child's body becomes accustomed to the drug, such effects will disappear. However, it is a good idea to call your doctor if any side effect in the gastrointestinal system persists for more than three days. Diarrhea can be managed by increasing the child's fluids to replace those that are being lost. Do not use a diarrhea remedy. If diarrhea follows use of an antibiotic, you can try feeding your child yogurt to replace beneficial bacteria that the antibiotic has removed from the intestine. Constipation can also be handled by increasing your child's fluid intake to up to six glasses of water a day. Extra water helps soften the stool and relieve the constipation. If your child complains of an upset stomach, check with your doctor to see if the prescribed drug can be given with food or milk. Often this will prevent stomach pain or nausea. Sucking on ice chips will relieve a dry mouth.

- Drowsiness is also a common side effect. If your child becomes drowsy, do not allow him or her to engage in activities requiring alertness and concentration. This includes bicycle riding, climbing, using skateboards, and working with machinery or potentially dangerous equipment.
- A headache should be reported to your doctor. It usually is not a serious side effect, but it is better to be on the safe side.
- If your child experiences a stuffy nose after taking a drug, ask your doctor if you can use nose drops or spray. If your child's throat is dry, try a simple salt gargle (½ teaspoon salt to 8 ounces of water). If your child develops a sore throat or a fever a few days after starting a drug, call your doctor. This could be a sign that the drug has affected the body's immune system and an infection has set in.
- Some drugs can lead to photosensitivity, that is, unusual sensitivity to the sun. Tetracycline, an antibiotic, is one such drug. If your child takes a dose of this type of drug and then remains exposed to the sun for even 10 minutes, he or she may receive a severe sunburn. Doctors often prescribe tetracycline for teen-age acne. Many teens with acne have discovered that some exposure to the sun helps their acne. But don't mix the two; that is, do not permit your teen to take tetracycline and then sunbathe. This does not mean your child cannot go outside, but he or she should be fully covered and should use a protective sunscreen.
- Skin reactions such as itching, swelling, or a rash may indicate an allergy to a drug. If your child develops any of these symptoms, call your doctor immediately. You may have to change drugs.

Hidden Side Effects

Some side effects have no symptoms, but instead affect the body without the person's being aware of it. When this is known about a drug, your doctor may want to monitor your child's progress with laboratory tests. If your child is taking such a drug for a prolonged time, periodic testing may become a necessary precaution.

Anaphylactic Shock

Anaphylactic shock is an extremely dangerous, life-threatening allergic reaction to a medication. It can also occur following an insect sting. It is absolutely essential that immediate medical treatment for it be obtained.

Onset of symptoms of anaphylactic shock are apparent almost immediately after the offending medication is given or the insect sting occurs. If the reaction follows the injection of a medication, it will probably be a drug that a physician has just given, so it is likely that medical treatment will still be readily available. However, you and your child could already have left the doctor's office before the first symptoms become apparent or before the child takes the first dose by mouth.

Symptoms: General uneasiness and flushed face followed by any or all of these rapidly developing conditions: skin welts (hives), itching skin, rapid heartbeat, breathing difficulty, sneezing, coughing, throbbing in the ears, vomiting, bowel and urine incontinence, convulsions. Shock, characterized by cold, clammy skin, weak and rapid pulse, and faintness, follow within a few minutes.

Treatment: *Call an ambulance or emergency life squad immediately.* Professional treatment is essential. While waiting, have the child lie down with his or her feet elevated.

A FINAL WORD

Always remember that when you give your child a medication, you are putting a chemical into the child's body. Sometimes the body tries to reject this chemical or reacts in a way that is uncomfortable. Occasionally, the reaction is so serious as to outweigh any benefits of the drug. Therefore, if your child displays any unusual symptoms or markedly different behavior after starting a drug and you are uncertain about its importance, call your doctor. When you are dealing with chemicals in the body, it is always prudent to be safe.

10

TREATING COMMON PROBLEMS

Fortunately, most of the illnesses that your child will have will be minor and can be treated at home. But how do you know when you can handle a problem and when you should call your doctor?

DEFINING THE PROBLEM

As your child grows from infancy through childhood and into adolescence you will observe, care for, and tend to your son or daughter. You as a parent probably know your child better than anyone else. For this reason, you will be able to recognize when your child is coming down with something. As the illness develops, you will monitor his or her condition and help your child cope. Because you know your child so well, you will probably be able to sense when the illness no longer can be managed at home without help from your health care provider. Naturally, if you have any questions or any doubts about treating your child's condition, you should call your doctor or health care provider right away.

As a general rule, however, you yourself can usually treat mild coughs and colds, vomiting, diarrhea, diaper rash, and even such a disease as chicken pox. Of course, there are exceptions, and if complications occur, you will need to call for medical assistance.

WHEN TO CALL THE DOCTOR

A cardinal rule that you should always remember is "Trust your own judgment." Suppose your child has a cold that you have been treating successfully with home remedies, but you don't feel that the child is responding to the treatment as well as he or she should. Furthermore, even though you can't put your finger on anything specific, the child just doesn't look right. Call your doctor. What may seem to be a minor cold could be masking a more serious illness, and sometimes your feeling that the child "just doesn't seem right" is the only clue to that illness. So don't hesitate to telephone your doctor about what may be a vague feeling of unease about your child.

In addition, as you will see in the following pages, some minor illnesses are not always quite so minor after all. For example, a bout of diarrhea—loose, watery bowel movements—for a 10-year-old may be only a short-lived and minor inconvenience, perhaps the result of eating too many ears of corn at yesterday's picnic. However, diarrhea in a baby can be potentially very dangerous, because it can lead to a serious loss of body fluids, a condition called *dehydration*. Thus, you should always ask your doctor for instructions about treating your baby or very young child for diarrhea.

Each of the following sections on common illnesses will provide you with suggestions for treating the problem yourself as well as offer guidelines about when to call your doctor.

FEVER

Fever is a very common sign of illness. Parents often have many questions about the nature of fever, what it signifies, whether it should be reduced, and, if so, how.

A fever is a rise in body temperature above the normal range, which is 98.6 to 99.8°F. In general, a body temperature over 101.5°F when measured with a rectal thermometer and above 100.5°F when measured with an oral thermometer is considered a fever.

Fever is not only a sign of illness; it is also a defense mechanism. During an illness, the temperature regulation center in the brain, which ordinarily maintains normal body temperature despite changes in the external environment, may respond to the illness by raising the body's temperature. The increase is thought to be a defense mechanism since the virus or other organisms causing the illness may not survive the higher body temperature. Although any disorder that affects the brain's temperature control center may cause a fever, by far the most common causes are infections, such as colds, influenza, and intestinal infections.

You should understand that the degree of fever does not necessarily indicate the severity of the illness. Some young children develop high fevers during minor illnesses. On the other hand, some serious conditions cause only a low-grade fever. Therefore, the severity of the illness cannot always be determined by the degree of the fever.

In some cases, the child's age is also a factor. In other words, a high fever in a child of a certain age may be more likely to signify a serious disease or infection than a similar fever in a child at a different age. As a general guideline, consult your doctor if

- your child is less than three months old, and the fever is greater than 101°F (38.3°C);
- your child is between seven and 24 months old, and the fever is greater than 103°F (39.5°C);
- your child has a fever greater than 105°F (41.0°C) no matter how old he or she is;
- your child has a fever—even a low one—that lasts more than five days.

Should You Treat a Fever?

If a fever is a defense mechanism, should you attempt to lower it? Most doctors feel that you should try to lower a fever over 101°F because at that temperature children feel uncomfortable. Do not confuse a fever and the illness causing the fever, however. Don't assume that when you lower a fever you are treating the underlying illness. Fever is a symptom, not an illness, and you are only lowering the fever to make the child more comfortable. The primary goal is to discover and treat the cause of the fever. Remember, too, that aggressively lowering the fever may mask the cause of the underlying illness. In such cases you may want to consult your doctor about his or her preference in lowering fever before a diagnosis has been made.

How to Lower a Fever

The primary treatment method that has been proven to be effective is the use of aspirin or acetaminophen to reduce the fever pharmaceutically. Although both are effective, there is a difference; aspirin is likely to irritate the lining of the stomach, and it can change the clotting properties of the blood. Furthermore, aspirin has been linked with a serious and possibly fatal condition called Reye's syndrome (see Chapter 5) that may follow a virus infection such as influenza and chicken pox. Although there is no firm proof that aspirin causes Reye's syndrome, you should avoid giving your child or teen-ager aspirin if you suspect flu or chicken pox.

Fortunately, acetaminophen has not been associated with this syndrome. Therefore, acetaminophen may become the cornerstone of your treatment of fever. Because a fever may appear before you can be certain that the illness is neither influenza nor chicken pox, you would be well advised to begin treatment using acetaminophen. Another advantage of acetaminophen is that it is available in liquid forms and thus is easier to administer to your child. However, don't confuse the liquid elixir and the drops; the drops contain over three times more of the active ingredient than the elixir.

The dosage you should give to reduce fever depends on your child's age and weight. See the table in Chapter 5 for dosage recommendations.

On a cautionary note, never attempt to lower a fever by rubbing down the child with alcohol. Not only can the fumes be irritating, but the child can also become chilled. The same precaution applies to ice water. If your child's fever is very high, sponging or bathing the child with lukewarm water can effectively reduce the fever to about 102°F.

When a child has a fever, he or she should not be covered or dressed too warmly. A light blanket or clothing is sufficient. The body needs to be able to throw off heat in a natural attempt to cool itself. Heavy clothing or blankets work against the body's natural self-defense.

PAIN

Like fever, pain is often a defense mechanism. It may force the body to slow down, thus protecting the damaged part of the body from overuse, and it may pinpoint the location of an injury or infection. Nevertheless, the discomfort can and should be reduced if at all possible.

Naturally, severe pain with or without other symptoms such as those listed in the accompanying table warrants an immediate call to the doctor. However, minor pain caused by an injury or accompanying an ordinary illness can be handled by you at home.

It is helpful to understand how pain occurs in the body. When a part of the body is injured, the injured cells produce special chemicals called *prostaglandins*. These chemicals produce inflammation, including heat, swelling, and redness.

The body's nerves carry the injury message to the brain, which processes the message and translates it into the perception of pain. The objective of pain treatment, then, is to block the production of prostaglandins or block the ability to perceive pain. Aspirin is one medication that works both ways. It acts primarily by preventing the injured cells from producing prostaglandins at the site of the injury, but it also affects a part of the brain called the *hypothalamus*.

Another category of drugs, narcotics, works principally on the nervous system by decreasing the sensitivity of the brain and by acting on the nerve endings at the site of the injury. Acetaminophen also relieves pain, but it does not block the production of prostaglandins. Nevertheless, it can be used if your child does not tolerate aspirin or you suspect that your child's pain symptoms are caused by influenza or chicken pox, for which you should not use aspirin. (See Chapter 5 for dosage recommendations for aspirin and acetaminophen.) A narcotic drug, most commonly codeine, is a prescription

Assessing the Severity of Pain

Call your doctor immediately if your child displays pain with these additional symptoms.

Pain	Accompanying Circumstances
Abdominal pain	Bloody vomiting, or bloody or black stools; recent abdominal injury; suspicion of drug overdose or of having swallowed poison; severe pain and cramping.
Chest pain	Shortness of breath.
Headache	Repeated vomiting; purple rash; visual impairment; stiff neck; irritability or lethargy; severe, sharp pain.
Sore throat	Shortness of breath; drooling.

medicine, and your doctor will give you instructions regarding its dosage and use.

For a minor injury, you might want to try rest and ice on the affected part before giving medication. For swelling and pain of a bump or bruise, you can put crushed ice in a plastic bag wrapped in a towel and place it on the affected area for 10 minutes at a time. Naturally, your child should not be using the injured part so that it can rest. Be careful not to leave the ice pack on too long, and use it only during the first 24 hours following the injury. Later, in a day or so, you can place warm clothes or heat on the injured part to increase blood flow and thus promote healing.

One final thought on the treatment of pain: don't forget the emotional impact of pain. Pain, even minor pain, can be frightening to a young child. You must acknowledge that pain is difficult to experience yet not become overwrought. Most of all, don't stare with horror at your child's cut lip. Most children take their cues from their parents, and if

you remain calm and reassuring, the child will follow suit—
and this demeanor and attitude may even reduce the pain
somewhat.

COMMON COLD

A cold is an infection of the upper respiratory tract caused
by one of over 185 viruses. A cold can affect the throat, the
nose, and possibly the eyes and ears. Do not confuse the
complications of a cold with the cold itself. The common
cold is not the same as a middle-ear infection, croup, pneumonia, or bronchitis. All of these can, however, follow a
cold, and a child with a cold is more susceptible to such
complications than one without a cold.

Because a cold is caused by one of many viruses, it is
impossible to develop a vaccine against the cold. An attack
by any virus causes the person to become immune to that
virus but not to any others. To protect against the 185 viruses
that can cause a cold, your child would need about 185
vaccinations. Since a cold is self-limiting—that is, it will
disappear of its own accord in a matter of days—it seems like
overkill to develop vaccines for such a minor illness.

This is not to say, however, that a cold does not produce
discomfort. Besides physical discomfort, a cold can make a
child irritable, cranky, and difficult to live with. Therefore,
parents often want to treat a cold to help the child and
preserve their own sanity. Nevertheless, always remember
that when you treat a cold you are relieving the symptoms
and not treating the disorder because a virus infection can be
cured only by time, not by medication, including antibiotics.

To treat a cold in general, give the child plenty of fluids
and have him or her rest. Bed rest is usually not necessary,
but strenuous activities should be curtailed. Use a cool mist
vaporizer to humidify the air and relieve nasal congestion. It
is a good idea to place the vaporizer in the child's room at
night to ease breathing while he or she is in a reclining
position. Also, do not be surprised if your child has little
appetite. Don't force him or her to eat, but encourage a
nutritious diet by offering light meals and small helpings.

Finally, if there is an infant or an elderly person in your home, you should try to isolate the child with the cold from the rest of the family. Both of those age groups are particularly vulnerable to colds and their complications.

Other than these general measures, you can treat the symptoms of a cold at home in most cases if you feel the child is uncomfortable or needs relief. Earlier in this chapter you read about treating a fever. In the following sections are some guidelines for treating the various symptoms of a cold. Remember, try to treat or relieve each individual symptom with a medication that is aimed at that symptom; in other words, when buying OTC cold medicines, buy single action products whenever possible. Why use a product that is both a decongestant and a fever reducer if your child does not need a decongestant?

Stuffy Nose

A stuffy nose results from a cold virus directly attacking the nose and its blood vessels. The cells in the nose secrete increased amounts of mucus, and the blood vessels become congested or filled with blood. Often, body chemicals called *histamines* accelerate these effects. The end result is that nasal passages are swollen shut, the nose runs with excess mucus, and the child has difficulty breathing.

To treat these effects you can try to shrink or decongest the blood vessels, and you can attempt to block the histamines from facilitating the effects. Therefore, you can choose a decongestant or an antihistamine. There are three main categories of decongestants:

1. pseudoephedrine (trade name Sudafed), available in liquid or tablets
2. phenylpropanolamine (trade name Dimetapp), a liquid
3. oxymetazoline (trade name Afrin) and xylometazoline (trade name Neo-Synephrine II), administered as nasal sprays

Both pseudoephedrine and phenylpropanolamine, whose effects can last from six to eight hours, can have side effects. When given by mouth, their effects can be systemwide. If side effects occur, you will notice changes in your child's behavior. Some children become extremely active; others may become drowsy or lethargic. Since the reaction depends on the makeup of the child's body, you can't predict in advance how your child will react to these medications. Therefore, it is wise to give them for the first time during the daytime so that you can observe your child and assess his or her reaction. It is very upsetting to have a child react to a medication by becoming overly active at nine o'clock in the evening when you are trying to put the child to bed. Phenylpropanolamine has also been found to cause higher blood pressure in adults, but this effect has not been proved in children. It may also result in a loss of appetite.

If you give any of these medications as a nasal spray, the side effects will not be as profound on the rest of the body. However, even this mode of administration has a major problem—the rebound effect. That is to say that while the medicine acts effectively for a period of time by constricting the blood vessels within the nasal passages, thus expanding the airway, eventually the walls of the vessels tire and begin to relax even beyond their normal state. The result after about three days can be greater congestion than before you began administering the medicine.

Oxymetazoline and xylometazoline are available only as nasal sprays and have the advantage of (1) exerting minimal effect on the rest of the body and (2) exerting their therapeutic effect for eight to 12 hours. However, the rebound effect is especially noticeable. These medications should never be used for more than three days.

The use of decongestants is controversial among medical professionals. Because of the side effects and the rebound effect, many think using a decongestant is not worth the disadvantages associated with its use. Other doctors, and some parents, feel that for certain children the decongestant's ability to ease breathing is worth risking the side effects. Incidentally, there is no conclusive evidence that a decongestant can dry up a runny nose; many people may believe this to be true because the decongestion of the nose that allows for easier breathing gives the impression of having dried up the mucus secretion. Perhaps the best move for you is to try a decongestant during the day. and attempt to evaluate your child's reaction to the medication. If you see positive results without unusually negative side effects, you may want to continue the use of the medicine.

The other medication commonly used for nasal congestion is an antihistamine. Its goal is to block the effect of the body chemicals called *histamines* on the congestion of blood vessels and the production of mucus. It is not known how effective antihistamines are in relieving a stuffy nose, but they seem fairly effective in drying up mucus secretions in the nose. However, antihistamines also have side effects. The most common one is drowsiness, but some children react by becoming overactive. A child taking an antihistamine can also develop dry mouth and nose and experience a loss of appetite.

Many antihistamines are marketed in combination with a decongestant. It has not been proven conclusively that this combination is any better than either medication alone. And remember, giving your child a combination medication increases the chances that a side effect will occur.

Sore Throat

A sore throat is usually an irritation of the throat caused by a virus (most often) or bacteria. The sore throat and typical accompanying symptoms of fever, headache, and difficulty in swallowing may be the same whether the cause is viral or bacterial. However, a bacterial infection may become dangerous or lead to serious complications. Thus, most doctors recommend that a child with a sore throat that lasts more than a day be seen by a medical professional.

The most common bacterial infection is caused by a strain of streptococci bacteria; you've probably heard the condition referred to as "strep throat." Untreated, strep throat may lead to other complications such as kidney or heart infection, but fortunately these complications are increasingly rare. Nonetheless, it is a good idea to have a throat culture done to determine if the sore throat is caused by a bacterium or a virus. If indeed the problem is strep throat, the doctor will give your child an antibiotic—either a penicillin or, in the case of a penicillin allergy, erythromycin. Don't be surprised or concerned if your doctor prefers to await the culture results before administering the antibiotic. The results usually are

When Sore Throat Warrants a Doctor's Visit

Take your child to the doctor if his or her sore throat is accompanied by any of the following symptoms, which may indicate a serious illness or complication:

- Swollen or tender neck glands
- persistent difficulty in swallowing
- breathing difficulty
- chest pain
- stiff neck
- earache
- pus discharge from nose or ears
- rash—purple-red or small, slightly raised red spots
- weakness
- prolonged vomiting
- confusion

If a sore throat worsens after 24 to 26 hours, call your doctor.

available within 24 hours, although there is a newer test that is faster. It will not be detrimental to your child to wait for that length of time. Besides, if the culture indicates that it is not a bacterial infection, your child will not need an antibiotic.

What can you do to help your child cope with a sore throat, whether it is caused by bacteria or viruses? Most children like cold liquids or ice cream. Nonacidic juices are welcome, too, as are Popsicles. Sometimes aspirin or acetaminophen will ease the pain. If you are unsure at the onset of a sore throat about the kind of illness the child is developing, you should use acetaminophen because of the link of aspirin to Reye's syndrome following flu or chicken pox. Older children might try gargling with saltwater (½ teaspoon salt to eight ounces of warm, not hot, water). Saltwater will not kill any germs, but it might soothe the soreness. Some older children obtain some relief from throat lozenges containing menthol, but young children cannot use these because of the danger of choking. Even older children should not take a throat lozenge while they are in bed or going to sleep. Overall, cold liquids are the best home remedy.

Cough

Coughing is a defense mechanism. It is the body's method of removing irritating or harmful matter that enters the breathing system. A cough is as serious as the condition that is causing it. To eliminate the cough, it is best to eliminate the disease or condition setting off the coughing.

You may wonder sometimes what you should do about a cough while the underlying condition is being treated. In light of the fact that coughing is a beneficial defense mechanism, sometimes it is better not to try to suppress it. Allow the body to protect and correct itself. On the other hand, if the cough is hard and frequent, the child may not be able to sleep and his or her muscles may become sore. In this case, you may want to consider a cough suppressant, especially at night when the child needs sleep.

Cough suppressants reduce the frequency of the cough by suppressing the cough reflex in the cough center in the brain. They may be narcotic (codeine) or nonnarcotic (dextromethorphan hydrobromide, trade name Benylin DM). Both are effective in treating a cough, but codeine can have a sedative effect on your child, which may or may not be desirable. Codeine is also a prescription medication. Dextromethorphan hydrobromide is as effective as codeine, and because it is nonnarcotic, it is not habit forming and can be given more frequently.

Other medications often suggested for coughs are decongestants, which may help dry up the nasal mucus that may be causing the cough. Antihistamines are also recommended for this purpose and when the cough is a byproduct of an allergy. Older children may find some relief from cough drops (Vick's Formula 44 Cough Control Discs), but young children, of course, cannot use them.

If you do treat your child's cough with medication and the medication does not seem to be helping, then discontinue using it. There is no reason to have the child take medicine that is not working. Don't forget, too, that a cough may be a sign of a serious illness, such as pneumonia, asthma, bronchitis, or whooping cough. If your child seems to become worse, his or her fever goes up, and/or he or she coughs up yellow material from the throat and chest, contact your doctor. Other precautions for the use of cough medicine:

- Do not give cough medicine to a child who is having difficulty breathing; call your doctor.
- Do not give cough medicine to a child with croup, an infection of the voice box (larynx) characterized by a tight barking or crowing cough.
- Do not give cough medicine to a child who may have inhaled a foreign object, including a cough drop or lozenge; administer first aid for choking.

CHICKEN POX

Chicken pox is one of the last childhood illnesses for which a vaccine has not been developed. However, a vaccine is now being tested and may be available soon. Chicken pox is a mild viral infection that is treated at home. Your doctor need not become involved unless there are complications or a secondary infection of the rash.

Chicken pox may begin with the symptoms of a cold, but most often the first sign is the distinctive rash. Each pox resembles an insect bite as it appears. Shortly, within hours, a small clear blister develops in the center of each spot. The blister usually breaks and is replaced by a small scab. New spots appear one at a time throughout each day for three or four days. Usually the spots crust and begin to heal in another three or four days. Your child is contagious from 24 hours before the rash appears until all the blisters have dried.

The rash usually begins on the chest or abdomen and moves outward to the arms and legs. However, it can begin anywhere, and before the illness is over your child may have pox anywhere on the skin and in the mucous membranes of

Precautions to Observe When Treating Chicken Pox

Chicken pox is normally a mild viral disease that is easily treated and causes a child only moderate discomfort. There are, however, some precautions to observe while letting the disease run its course:

- Do not use aspirin.
- If high fever, faintness or collapse, vomiting, headache, and convulsions occur, call your doctor.
- The lymph glands of the body, found in the neck, armpits, and groin, usually swell during chicken pox attacks, but if they become red and sore, they may be infected. Contact your doctor.
- If bruises with no known causes appear on the skin, call your doctor.
- If the pox become redder and sore and form pus, call your doctor. This may be an infection that should be treated with an antibiotic (which will not affect the course of the chicken pox, only the infection).
- Chicken pox is dangerous to anyone, child or unprotected adult, who is taking steroid drugs or any drugs that suppress the immune system. It is also dangerous to persons with immune deficiencies that inhibit that person's ability to fight disease. If yours is such a child, call your doctor at the first sign of chicken pox. If your normal child develops chicken pox and you know other people with these conditions, isolate your child from them.
- Chicken pox is also dangerous to newborns. If your newborn contracts chicken pox or is exposed to it, call your doctor.

the mouth, genitals, anus, and eyelids. The most distinctive feature of the rash is its extreme itchiness.

Chicken pox symptoms that you should know how to manage at home are fever and itchiness of the rash. First, do not treat the fever with aspirin. Aspirin has been linked to Reye's syndrome, a serious complication of chicken pox. Acetaminophen is safe to use during chicken pox. Also, many warnings about aspirin and Reye's syndrome use the word *children,* but lately many of the cases of Reye's syndrome have been teen-agers. So if your pre-teen or teen-ager contracts chicken pox, do not use aspirin.

The rash is often more troublesome to the child than the fever. The itching can be very intense, and the child may have an overwhelming desire to scratch. If the scabs are scratched off, a scar will form, so you should attempt to relieve the itching. A lukewarm to cool bath will bring some relief. Some parents have found that adding cornstarch to the water helps. A warm bath will intensify the itching while the child is in the water, but the itching will be lessened considerably after the bath. Remember to pat the child dry gently to avoid disturbing the scabs or breaking the blisters. You can also apply calamine lotion to the rash. However, do not use calamine lotion with phenol; it is too irritating to the pox spots. Trim the child's nails, and stress to an older child the consequences of scratching.

VOMITING

Although vomiting may be a sign of a serious illness, especially if it is persistent and prolonged, most bouts of vomiting, like fever and coughing, are defense mechanisms to rid the body of irritating substances. For a young child, vomiting may indicate an intolerance to milk, formula, or another food. In a child of any age, vomiting may indicate an infection of the intestinal tract or even a simple overload. You will soon learn how your child's digestive system works and then be able to interpret what the vomiting means. Incidentally, many babies "spit up" milk and partially digested food as a response to a full stomach; it takes time for their digestive systems to develop a strong muscle at the top of the stomach to prevent the food from coming up when the stomach muscles contract. This is a matter of physical maturity and not a symptom of illness. Later, as your baby grows older, he or she may experience his or her first vomiting episode. Don't be surprised if the child is not only extremely surprised but also extremely frightened. Vomiting is a disagreeable experience at best, but for a young child the physical symptoms of this phenomenon are unexpected and can be scary. Reassurance and comfort are important in the home treatment for vomiting.

Your main objective in treating vomiting is to prevent a severe loss of body fluids, or dehydration. Dehydration can become dangerous, especially in a young baby, because excessive loss of fluids is accompanied by excessive loss of body salts, which disturbs the body's chemistry. Therefore, you should attempt to replace the fluids. Give the child soothing sips of cold, clear liquids—ice, water, carbonated drinks, flavored gelatin water, diluted apple juice, or—if your doctor agrees—commercial mineral or electrolyte mixtures (Pedialyte or Lytren). The commercial mixtures contain body salts. Do not give your child milk, orange or other citrus juices, solid food, or aspirin. All are hard for an upset stomach to digest and are likely to provoke more vomiting.

The best way to give the fluids is to offer small amounts frequently, which the child is more likely to keep down than large amounts. You can start with one to two ounces every 15

Symptoms of Dehydration

- infrequent urination
- decreased amounts of urine
- drowsiness
- sunken eyes
- sunken soft spot in baby's skull
- rapid or slow breathing
- dry mouth
- skin remains rigid when pinched gently

minutes. If this works, you can lengthen the intervals and increase the amount. If it doesn't work, you may have to offer a teaspoon every five to ten minutes. If a child can keep even this small amount down, he or she will retain about two ounces an hour. If the child cannot keep anything at all down, call your doctor.

When the child seems better, you can graduate to a bland, nonmilk, nonfat diet. Offer bananas, toast or dry crackers, apples or applesauce, and rice. Don't be in too much of a hurry, however, to progress to solid foods. Too rapid advancement may cause a relapse. Don't be too concerned about your child not eating solid foods for a couple of days. He or she will catch up when the stomach is ready.

Normally, you can manage vomiting at home. However, if you do not know what is causing the vomiting, you should check with your doctor. Also watch for signs of a headache, fever, or abdominal pain. These symptoms along with the vomiting should be brought to the attention of your doctor. Also contact the doctor if the vomiting does not respond to your treatment after two days or if your child seems dehydrated. To check for dehydration, pinch the skin on the back of the child's hand and observe whether there is a time lapse before the skin smooths out again. If a small ridge of skin remains raised momentarily after the pinch, the child may be dehydrated since the decreased moisture in the skin reduces the elasticity of the skin and therefore the skin's ability to spring back. (Check the accompanying list for other signs of dehydration.) At this point your doctor may choose to give the child fluids intravenously in the hospital.

DIARRHEA

Diarrhea refers to loose, watery bowel movements, not to the frequency of bowel movements. Depending on the cause of diarrhea, the child may also experience cramps, loss of appetite, fever, and vomiting. If there is vomiting, treat the vomiting first and then treat the diarrhea.

Diet for Diarrhea

- commercial mineral and electrolyte solutions
- flavored gelatin water
- flavored gelatin
- diluted beef bouillon
- small amounts of lean beef or lamb
- boiled chicken
- soft- or hard-boiled egg
- cooked rice
- dry baked or boiled potato
- fresh banana
- fresh apple
- toast or crackers and jelly

The home treatment for diarrhea is essentially the same as for vomiting. The main goal is to replace body fluids that are lost because of the diarrhea. As with vomiting, check for dehydration (see the list of symptoms of dehydration).

Limit your child to clear fluids at first. As the diarrhea begins to subside, you can start to introduce some solid foods such as those in the list below. Do not give the child milk. Also avoid foods with roughage (whole grains and nuts, for example), vegetables and fruits (except apples and bananas), butter, fatty meats, and peanut butter.

There are several over-the-counter medications intended to treat diarrhea. They contain a clay derivative (kaolin) and an extract from citrus fruit (pectin). The most commonly known brand is Kaopectate. Neither kaolin nor pectin is harmful, but they are not particularly helpful either. They are designed to thicken and firm up the stool, but the frequency, amount, and resulting water loss of the bowel movements remain unchanged. Therefore, many doctors do not recommend such medication because the parent giving the medicine may be lulled into thinking the child is improving and not watch for signs of dehydration.

A few prescription drugs treat diarrhea, but they have side

effects that may make the diarrhea worse in a child. They are not recommended for children.

If your child's condition shows no improvement after two days, contact your doctor.

CONSTIPATION

Constipation refers to stools that are too hard. It does not mean that bowel movements are infrequent. Do not assume your child is constipated if he or she has a normal soft bowel movement every other day or even every third or fourth day.

Constipation occurs in the large intestine. The job of the large intestine is to absorb water from the liquid waste material it receives from the small intestine. If the intestine absorbs too much water, the stool becomes too hard. There are two main reasons why children's intestines may sometimes absorb too much water. First, the child is not eating enough roughage, which holds water in the stools. Second, the child resists or puts off the impulse to move his or her bowels. Often, this occurs if the parent is putting too much pressure on the child during toilet training. Once the stools become hard, moving the bowels becomes painful, leading to further postponement. The hard stool also enlarges the intestine, weakening the muscle tone, and the impulse to empty the intestine diminishes. This cycle can lead to chronic constipation.

How can you cope with constipation at home? You should first change the child's diet. Include more bulk and fiber, such as can be found in the list of foods below. At the same time, decrease the proportion of constipating foods in your child's diet, such as milk and bananas. Within two to five days the constipation should be under control. A precautionary word: make the changes in a gradual manner and with small amounts at a time. In some children large amounts of bulk and fiber can lead to diarrhea.

If the constipation is a direct result of toilet training, stop the training temporarily. If your child is postponing natural urges for another reason, attempt to find out the reason and take measures to correct the situation.

Diet to Treat and Prevent Constipation

- all fruits (except bananas and apples), especially if eaten with their skins on
- all vegetables, especially if eaten raw (except peeled potatoes)
- whole grain cereals and breads
- unrefined sugars—honey, molasses, brown sugar

Laxatives are not the answer. You should not give your child a laxative; they can be habit-forming and should not be used on a regular basis. Furthermore, a laxative may force a painful bowel movement, leading the child to hold back even more. Enemas and glycerine suppositories stimulate the emptying of the last few inches of the large intestine. However, like laxatives, they can be habit-forming. Nevertheless, a doctor may occasionally suggest their temporary or one-time use to reestablish a bowel movement routine.

DIAPER RASH

A diaper rash is an irritation of the skin in the diaper area. It is very common; almost all babies have a diaper rash at one point or another.

There are various causes of diaper rashes, and it is often necessary to pinpoint the cause so that the proper treatment can be used. Simple diaper rashes result when the skin reacts to the presence of urine or feces in the diaper area. An ammonia rash, for example, develops when the skin is burned by the ammonia formed when the urine is broken down by normal skin bacteria. This often occurs after the child has been asleep for a long time without a diaper change.

The skin may also be irritated by chemicals used in washing cloth diapers—soap, detergent, fabric softener, or bleach.

Or the skin may be irritated by the chemicals used to manufacture disposable diapers. The outer plastic cover on disposable diapers as well as plastic or rubber pants worn over diapers may also be an irritant. In addition, these plastic coverings trap heat and moisture in the diaper, thus increasing the possibility of a rash.

Sometimes diaper rash is caused by diarrhea, an allergy to a food or drug, a skin infection, or a disease that involves a rash all over the body (chicken pox, for instance). If you can't detect the characteristic smell of ammonia, try to pinpoint the cause by looking for other clues. Has the child had a new food or medicine lately? Are you using a new kind of diaper, or have you changed your laundering procedures? Does the baby have any other signs of illness?

Once you have discovered the reason for the rash, you can take steps to eliminate it. Keep the baby as dry as possible, changing his or her diapers frequently. Be certain to wash the skin at each changing. Avoid using plastic or rubber coverings, and if at all possible, expose the diaper area to the air for short periods of time. You can also apply a mild protective ointment or cream to prevent irritants in the urine or feces from reaching the skin. These ointments and creams include zinc oxide ointment, petroleum jelly and an ointment containing zinc oxide, cod liver oil, talc, petrolatum, and lanolin (trade name Desitin). Such ointments are often very helpful, but you should not use more than one of them at a time.

If you suspect a new food is causing the reaction, do not give it to the child. If you've introduced several new foods, stop all of them and gradually reintroduce them one at a time so that you can determine which one is the culprit. Incidentally, it is always a good idea when giving new foods to a baby to start them one at a time. That way you'll know immediately if the baby has a reaction to them.

You can also check the methods of laundering the diapers. Sometimes rinsing them twice takes care of the problem. Some parents find that rinsing diapers in a diluted acid (one ounce of vinegar to one gallon of water) reduces the irritating alkalinity of detergent and soap residues.

If the rash does not begin to clear up within two days, call your doctor. A yeast infection of the skin could be the problem. In this case, your doctor may prescribe an antiyeast cream, most likely nystatin (Mycostatin). This drug is available in a cream, ointment, or powder. If the diaper rash is severe, ask your doctor about the powder form; it is easier to apply to swollen, raw skin.

Other infections will probably respond to antibiotic cream such as neomycin. Do not use steroid cream, however, without discussing it with your doctor. A steroid cream may even worsen a diaper rash if used without the appropriate antiyeast or antibacterial medication. Nevertheless, in some cases the doctor may suggest a 1% hydrocortisone cream to be used along with the other ointment. If used correctly, there should be no side effects.

If your treatment is correct, the diaper rash should improve in about a week. Sometimes complete disappearance of a severe rash may take a few weeks. If after that time the rash does not seem to be clearing up, call your doctor.

PART II

MEDICATION
PROFILES

In this section you will find descriptions, called *profiles*, of some medications commonly used for children. The profiles have been divided into two chapters: prescription drugs, for which your doctor must write a prescription, and over-the-counter products, which you can buy without a prescription. The medications are profiled in alphabetical order in Chapters 11 and 12 by the most common or familiar name. If you can't find the drug you're looking for, check the index; all equivalent products are cross-referenced there.

Each profile gives the most important information about a drug. By reading a drug's profile, you will learn what to expect from that drug, in terms of either its benefits or its adverse effects. Many parents prefer to read a drug's profile before filling a prescription so that they can clarify any points of confusion or ask knowledgeable questions of their pharmacist.

To use the profiles most efficiently, you should understand the significance of each category in the profile. Each prescription drug profile contains the following information:

- **Name of Drug.** Each drug is listed by either its brand name or its generic name, which is usually the name of its ingredient(s). When a product is generic, that is noted in parentheses following the medication name.
- **Ingredients.** This section lists the principal chemical components of the medication.

- **Equivalent Product(s).** This category lists all drugs that are chemically the exact same formulation as the drug being profiled. A general rule of thumb to remember is that brand names begin with a capital letter and generic names with a lower-case letter. If your doctor has prescribed a drug that is available generically, ask to have the prescription request the generic equivalent—it may be cheaper. Remember, however, that not all generic drugs are exactly equivalent to trade name drugs; you should ask your pharmacist about this.

- **Used For.** This section describes what the drug is prescribed for.

- **Dosage Form and Strength.** The forms of the drug (tablets, liquids, capsules, and so forth) are listed along with each form's strength or concentration of active ingredients. In a few cases, additional forms or strengths exist but are not recommended for use with children, so they are not listed here.

- **Storage.** This information enables you to store the drug properly for maximum effectiveness and safety.

- **Before Using This Medication, Tell Your Doctor.** This section tells you what your doctor needs to know about your individual child before a medication is prescribed or used. Some medications are the preferred choice of treatment for a certain illness, but they should not be used for a child with a history of asthma, as an example. The doctor must also know about any other drugs your child is currently taking and about any allergies or family history of allergies. *This information is extremely important.*

- **This Drug Should Not Be Used If.** Here you will learn when a drug should not be used and under what circumstances a drug's use is inappropriate or even hazardous.

- **How to Use.** This section offers tips on administering the drug or a drug form to your child. You will learn whether you should give the drug on an empty stomach or with food. You will read about dosage intervals. In short, this category will help you give the medicine in the most effective and safe way.

- **Time Required for Drug to Take Effect.** Having this information will enable you to evaluate the effectiveness of the drug you are giving your child.

- **Missing a Dose.** This section tells you what to do if you forget to give a dose to your child. Even with these guidelines, this is a question to ask your doctor so that you are absolutely sure of what to do in such a situation.
- **Symptoms of Overdose.** If your child takes too much medication or for some reason the drug accumulates in his or her body, the symptoms listed in this section will alert you to the danger of overdose. Many of these symptoms will also appear in the "Serious Adverse Reactions" section under "Side Effects."
- **Side Effects.** This category is divided into the two sections: "Minor and Expected" and "Serious Adverse Reactions."

  The minor side effects are those that are unavoidable and that also tend to disappear as your child's body grows accustomed to the drug. These side effects will not necessarily occur, but if they do, you will know that they are not too serious. On the other hand, if minor side effects persist or seem unusually severe, call your doctor. There is no sense in allowing your child to experience a side effect, no matter how minor, that is more uncomfortable than the symptoms the drug is supposed to be treating. Sometimes a change in dosage will eliminate these side effects.

  Those effects listed under "Serious Adverse Reactions" always warrant a call to your doctor. If you are giving your child a prescription drug and he or she experiences an adverse reaction, do not automatically stop administering the drug—sometimes stopping a drug suddenly is as dangerous as the adverse effects it is causing—but do call your doctor immediately. The doctor may have to weigh the benefit of the drug against the risk of its adverse effects. Again, too, perhaps changing the dosage will eliminate the problem.

- **Effects of Long-Term Use.** This information will make you aware of the drug's benefits versus its risks.
- **Habit-Forming Possibility.** This section informs you about the possibility of the child's developing a physical or psychological dependence on the drug.
- **Precautions and Suggestions.** This category is divided into three sections: "Foods and Beverages," "Other Medi-

cines, Prescription or OTC," and "Other," miscella-
neous information you should know about the drug. The
foods and beverages section tells you about any restrictions in regard to these items. Restrictions concerning
alcoholic beverages have not been included because this
is a book about children's medications. Nevertheless,
sometimes a child will be taking an over-the-counter
medication that contains alcohol. To be on the safe side,
always assume that alcohol will interact with any drug.
For children, this is a safe assumption. The other two
subsections of this category explain drug interactions and
other activities that may enhance or decrease the effects
of a drug. You will also find tips about using the drug.

If you ever have any doubts about how your child is
reacting to a medicine, call your doctor.

• **Medical Tests.** Here you will find out if a drug will
interfere with the results of a test or if your doctor will
want to perform medical tests on your child during the
drug therapy to monitor the progress. Don't forget to tell
anyone recommending or performing a medical test that
your child is taking medication. Also, don't forget about
dentists and other specialists and health care providers.

The over-the-counter drug profiles include most of the
same categories of information. Those categories referring to
specific treatment by a physician ("Before using this medication . . ." and "Medical tests") have been eliminated because they generally relate only to prescriptions or to physicians'
recommendations. The "Time required . . ." category does
not appear in this section because OTC medications are generally purchased to treat short-term symptoms of minor ailments, not the causes of the ailments themselves, as is more
often the case with prescription drugs. Again, it must be
emphasized that even with OTC products you must be alert to
your child's reactions. These profiles will help you, but
always call your health care provider if you question anything
about an OTC drug and its effect on your child.

11

PRESCRIPTION DRUGS

ACCUTANE

Ingredient(s): isotretinoin (13-*cis*-retinoic acid)

Equivalent Product(s): none

Used For: treating severe cystic acne

Dosage Form and Strength: capsules—10 mg, 20 mg, 40 mg

Storage: This drug is sensitive to light. Store in tight, light-resistant containers at room temperature.

Before Using This Medication Tell Your Doctor: if your child is taking minocycline or tetracycline or if you know or suspect that your teen-ager is pregnant or breast-feeding.

This Drug Should Not Be Used If: your teen-ager is, intends to be, or even thinks she is pregnant. This drug should not be used by persons who are allergic to the preservative parabens used in its formulation.

How to Use: Give with meals.

Time Required for Drug to Take Effect: 15 to 20 weeks

Missing a Dose: Because this drug is so powerful and the dosage is calculated carefully by your doctor, seek his or her specific instructions regarding missed doses.

Symptoms of Overdose: nausea, vomiting, severe and sudden headache, irritability, hair loss

Side Effects:

Minor and expected:
- inflammation of lips, dry skin, itching, eye irritation, conjunctivitis, dry nose and mouth, fatigue, indigestion, muscle pain and stiffness, nosebleed, temporary thinning of hair, sensitivity to sunlight

ACCUTANE (*continued*)

Serious adverse reactions (CALL YOUR DOCTOR):
- Vision problems, headache, nausea, vomiting, abdominal pain, severe diarrhea, rectal bleeding, weight loss

Effects of Long-Term Use: This drug may increase blood fat levels, especially in overweight or diabetic persons or in those with family histories of high fat levels. Blood levels return to normal when the drug is stopped.

Habit-Forming Possibility: none

Precautions and Suggestions:

Foods and beverages:
- Avoid alcoholic beverages.

Other Medicines, Prescription or OTC:
- Persons taking Accutane should not simultaneously take vitamin A supplements. This drug may also interact with the antibiotics minocycline or tetracycline.

Other:
- Accutane can cause an increased sensitivity to the sun. Those taking this drug should wear protective clothing and/or sunglasses while outside.
- A short-term worsening of the acne may occur, especially at the beginning of the therapy.
- During the healing of skin lesions there may occasionally be an unusual increase in the crusting of the lesions.
- Young women of childbearing age who are sexually active should have a pregnancy test before starting treatment with this drug. One month before, during, and one month after treatment an effective contraceptive should be used. Accutane has been linked to major birth defects.

Medical Tests: Accutane may affect the results of blood and urine tests.

AMOXIL

Ingredient(s): amoxicillin

Equivalent Product(s): amoxicillin (generic), Larotid, Polymox, Sumox, Trimox, Utimox, Wymox

Used For: treatment of bacterial infections, including infections of the ear, nose, throat, lower respiratory tract, skin, and genitourinary tract.

Dosage Form and Strength: capsules—250 mg, 500 mg; chewable tablets—125 mg, 250 mg; oral suspension—50 mg per 1 ml, 125 mg per 5 ml teaspoon, 250 mg per 5 ml teaspoon; drops—50 mg per ml

Storage: Keep liquid forms in the refrigerator. Store all forms in tightly closed containers.

Before Using This Medication Tell Your Doctor: about any asthmatic or allergic reaction your child has had to penicillin or any other antibiotics. Also, tell your doctor if your child is allergic by nature or has ever had hay fever, hives, skin rashes, or any other allergic reactions to anything. Inform your doctor if your child has ever been diagnosed as having liver or kidney problems. Be sure to tell your doctor about any other medicines (prescription or nonprescription) that your child is taking.

This Drug Should Not Be Used If: your child has had an allergic reaction to any form of penicillin or has had a previous reaction to Amoxil.

How to Use: Give Amoxil as directed by your doctor, usually at evenly spaced intervals around the clock. The drug can be taken with or without food. If you are using the oral suspension, shake the bottle well before measuring, and measure the dose with a marked or medical teaspoon— an ordinary kitchen teaspoon is not an accurate measure.

AMOXIL (continued)

If you are giving the drops to a baby or small child, measure the medicine in a marked dropper and release the solution directly into the inside of the child's cheek. The drops can also be mixed with formula, milk, fruit juice, water, or ginger ale and taken immediately. If you do this, you must be certain that the child swallows the entire drink to receive the full dose of medicine.

Time Required for Drug to Take Effect: usually two to five days, depending on the type and severity of infection being treated. However, continue giving the medication for the full time prescribed by your doctor even if your child seems well; otherwise, the infection may return.

Missing a Dose: Give the missed dose immediately, but if it is almost time for the next dose, wait to give the next dose until about halfway through the regular interval between doses. For example, if you are to give a dose at 8:00, 4:00, and 12:00 and you remember at 3:00 P.M. that you forgot the 8:00 A.M. dose, give the missed dose at 3:00 P.M. but wait until about 8:00 P.M. to give the 4:00 P.M. dose. Then return to your regular schedule at midnight. Do not skip a dose or double the dose.

Symptoms of Overdose: possible severe and persistent nausea, vomiting, and/or diarrhea

Side Effects:

Minor and expected:
- diarrhea, nausea

Serious adverse reactions (CALL YOUR DOCTOR):
- hives, itching, or skin rash; difficult breathing; fever; joint pain; sore throat; dark-colored tongue; yellow-green stools; sores in the mouth; severe and persistent nausea, vomiting, or diarrhea

AMOXIL (*continued*)

Effects of Long-Term Use: possibility of superinfection—that is, a second infection in addition to the infection being treated. A superinfection is caused by bacteria and other organisms that are not susceptible to or affected by the drug being used to treat the original infection. Thus, these organisms, which are normally too few in number to cause problems, grow unchecked and cause a second infection that may require a different drug to treat.

Habit-Forming Possibility: none

Precautions and Suggestions:

Foods and beverages:
• no restrictions

Other Medicines, Prescription or OTC:
• Antacids and other antibiotics reduce the absorption and effect of Amoxil.

Other:
• If mild diarrhea is a side effect, ask your doctor if you can give your child yogurt. The beneficial bacteria in yogurt replace the intestine's natural beneficial bacteria that have been reduced or eliminated by Amoxil.
• This drug should be given for the full length of time recommended by your doctor even if the child seems to have recovered. Otherwise, the infection may return and be more difficult to treat the second time.
• Do not use the medication beyond its expiration date on the label. As a general rule of thumb, discard after 14 days any unused liquid medication that has been refrigerated.

Medical Tests: Your doctor may recommend blood counts or liver or kidney function tests during treatment with this drug in order to monitor your child's progress. Any drug

AMOXIL (*continued*)

may affect the results and accuracy of a medical test. If a doctor recommends a medical or laboratory test for any condition, inform the doctor that your child is taking Amoxil before the test is performed.

AUGMENTIN

Ingredient(s): amoxicillin and potassium clavulanate

Equivalent Product(s): none

Used For: infections of the ear, throat, sinuses, skin and skin structure, lower respiratory tract, and urinary tract caused by bacteria that have become resistant to penicillin and other antibiotics

Dosage Form and Strength: tablets—250 mg amoxicillin, 125 mg potassium clavulanate; 500 mg amoxicillin, 125 mg potassium clavulanate; pediatric oral suspension—125 mg amoxicillin, 31.25 mg potassium clavulanate; 250 mg amoxicillin, 62.5 mg potassium clavulanate

Storage: Keep liquid forms of this medication in the refrigerator. Discard unused liquid after 14 days. Store all forms in tightly closed containers.

Before Using This Medication Tell Your Doctor: if your child is allergic to penicillin or has a history of diabetes or liver or kidney problems. Tell your doctor if your child has mononucleosis. Tell your doctor about any drugs, prescription or nonprescription, your child is taking and about any allergies your child has or any family history of allergies.

This Drug Should Not Be Used If: your child is allergic to any form of penicillin or has mononucleosis.

How to Use: Give Augmentin as directed by your doctor, usually every eight hours. This drug can be taken with or without food. If you are using the oral suspension, shake the bottle well before measuring the dose.

Time Required for Drug to Take Effect: usually two to five days, depending on the infection being treated. However, continue to give the medication for the full time

AUGMENTIN (continued)

your doctor has prescribed, even if your child seems
well; otherwise, the infection may return.

Missing a Dose: Give the missed dose immediately, but if it
is almost time for the next dose, wait to give the next
dose until about halfway through the regular interval
between doses. For example, if you are to give a dose at
8:00, 4:00, and 12:00 and you remember at 3:00 P.M.
that you forgot the 8:00 A.M. dose, give the missed dose
at 3:00 P.M. but wait until 8:00 P.M. to give the 4:00 P.M.
dose. Then return to the regular schedule. Do not skip a
dose or double the dose.

Symptoms of Overdose: possible severe and persistent nausea, vomiting, and/or diarrhea

Side Effects:

Minor and expected:
• diarrhea, nausea, vomiting, headache, stomach discomfort

Serious adverse reactions (CALL YOUR DOCTOR):
• hives, itching, or skin rash; difficult breathing; fever;
joint pain; sore throat; dark-colored tongue; yellow-
green stools; sores in the mouth; severe and persistent
nausea, vomiting, or diarrhea

Effects of Long-Term Use: superinfection—a second infection in addition to the infection being treated. The
superinfection is caused by bacteria and other organisms
that are not susceptible to or affected by the drug being
used to treat the original infection. Thus these organisms, which are normally too few in number to cause
problems, grow unchecked and cause a second infection
that may require a different drug to treat.

AUGMENTIN (*continued*)

Habit-Forming Possibility: none

Precautions and Suggestions:

Foods and beverages:
• no restrictions

Other Medicines, Prescription or OTC:
• Antacids and other antibiotics reduce the absorption and effect of Augmentin.

Other:
• If mild diarrhea is a side effect, ask your doctor if you can give your child yogurt. The beneficial bacteria in yogurt replace the intestine's natural beneficial bacteria that have been reduced or eliminated by Augmentin.
• This drug should be given for the full length of time recommended by your doctor even if the child seems to have recovered. Otherwise, the infection may return and be more difficult to treat the second time.
• Do not use the medication beyond its expiration date on the label. As a general rule of thumb, discard after 14 days any unused liquid medication that has been refrigerated.

Medical Tests: Your doctor may recommend tests during treatment with this drug, including blood counts and liver and kidney function tests, to monitor your child's progress. Any drug may affect the results and accuracy of a medical test. If a doctor recommends a medical or laboratory test for any condition, inform the doctor that your child is taking Augmentin.

BACTRIM

Ingredient(s): trimethoprim and sulfamethoxazole

Equivalent Product(s): Bethaprim, Cotrim, Septra, Sulfatrim, trimethoprim and sulfamethoxazole (generic)

Used For: treatment of infections, especially in the urinary tract, middle ear, lungs, or intestines

Dosage Form and Strength: tablets—80 mg trimethoprim, 400 mg sulfamethoxazole; 160 mg trimethoprim, 800 mg sulfamethoxazole; oral suspension—40 mg trimethoprim, 200 mg sulfamethoxazole per 5 ml (1 medical teaspoon)

Storage: Store at room temperature.

Before Using This Medication Tell Your Doctor: if your chid has liver or kidney disease, any vitamin deficiencies, severe allergies, bronchial asthma, or glucose-6-phosphate dehydrogenase deficiency. Also tell your doctor about any other drugs, prescription or nonprescription, your child is using.

This Drug Should Not Be Used If: your child is allergic to its ingredients or to sulfa drugs or if your child is anemic because of a vitamin deficiency. It should not be used for babies less than two months old. Bactrim should not be used to treat strep throat because it is not effective enough.

How to Use: Give each dose with a full glass of water. Give all the medication prescribed even if your child's symptoms disappear and he or she feels well. While taking this drug, your child should drink plenty of water—at least eight glasses each day.

Time Required for Drug to Take Effect: five to 14 days

Missing a Dose: Give the missed dose immediately. If it is almost time for the next dose, give that next dose mid-

BACTRIM (*continued*)

way through the interval between doses. Then return to the regular schedule. Do not skip a dose or double the dose.

Symptoms of Overdose: A maximum tolerated dose in humans is unknown. However, in studies in which amimals were given large doses of the drug, they developed tremors or convulsions, slowed breathing, reduced activity, and loss of muscular coordination.

Side Effects:

Minor and expected:
- abdominal pain, loss of appetite, nausea, diarrhea, dizziness, headache, vomiting, sensitivity to the sun, sore mouth

Serious adverse reactions (CALL YOUR DOCTOR):
- rash, mouth sores, unusual bleeding and bruising, sore throat, fever, paleness, skin discoloration, difficult urination, breathing difficulties, fluid retention, convulsions, ringing in ears, tingling in hands or feet, weakness, blood disorders, muscle weakness, kidney disorders

Effects of Long-Term Use: Possible reduction in the ability of the bone marrow, the soft connective tissue inside the bones, to do its job of manufacturing blood cells, thus leading to a deficiency of certain blood cells

Habit-Forming Possibility: none

Precautions and Suggestions:

Foods and beverages:
- no restrictions

Other Medicines, Prescription or OTC:
- Bactrim may react with phenytoin (Dilantin), antibiotics (oxacillin, penicillins), and para-aminobenzoic acid

BACTRIM (*continued*)

(PABA) found in sunscreens. Tell your doctor about any drugs your child is currently taking.

Other:
• This drug may cause your child to be sensitive to the sun. Be sure your child is not exposed to the sun and is protected by a sunscreen that does not contain PABA.

Medical Tests: Some doctors may suggest complete blood counts to monitor your child's progress. Bactrim can interfere with the results of some blood and urine tests.

CECLOR

Ingredient(s): cefaclor

Equivalent Product(s): none

Used For: treatment of bacterial infections

Dosage Form and Strength: capsules—250 mg, 500 mg; oral suspension—125 mg per 5 ml; 250 mg per 5 ml

Storage: Store liquid in refrigerator. Discard unused portion after 14 days. Store capsules in dry, tightly closed containers at room temperature.

Before Using This Medication Tell Your Doctor: if your child is allergic to any antibiotics, especially cephalosporins and penicillin. Also tell your doctor if your child has a history of kidney problems, colitis, or diabetes. Tell your doctor about any drugs, prescription or nonprescription, your child is taking and about any allergies your child has or any family history of allergies.

This Drug Should Not Be Used If: your child is allergic to its ingredient. It is not recommended for babies under one month of age.

How to Use: Give this drug at regularly spaced intervals around the clock. This drug can be given with or without food, but if upset stomach occurs, give the dose with food. Give the capsule with a full glass of water. If you are using the oral suspension, shake it well before measuring the dose. Give either dosage form for the full time recommended even if the child seems well.

Time Required for Drug to Take Effect: varies, depending on the infection being treated. Using the drug for two to five days is usually necessary to see if the drug is effective against the infection being treated.

CECLOR (*continued*)

Missing a Dose: Take the missed dose immediately. However, if it is almost time for your next dose, space the next dose about midway through the regular interval between doses. For example, if you are to give a dose at 8:00, 4:00, and 12:00 and you remember at 3:00 P.M. that you forgot the 8:00 A.M. dose, give the missed dose at 3:00 P.M. but wait until about 8:00 P.M. to give the 4:00 P.M. dose. Then return to the regular schedule. Do not skip a dose or double the dose.

Symptoms of Overdose: abdominal cramping, nausea, vomiting, diarrhea

Side Effects:

Minor and expected:
- upset stomach, nausea, diarrhea, loss of appetite, headache, dizziness, fatigue, sores in the mouth

Serious adverse reactions (CALL YOUR DOCTOR):
- severe diarrhea, rash, fever, itching, hives, joint pain, difficult breathing, genital itching, sore throat, tingling in hands and feet

Effects of Long-Term Use: superinfection—a second infection in addition to the infection being treated. A superinfection is caused by bacteria and other organisms that are not susceptible to or affected by the drug being used to treat the original infection. Thus, these organisms, which are normally too few in number to cause problems, grow unchecked and cause a second infection that may require a different drug to treat.

Habit-Forming Possibility: none

Precautions and Suggestions:

Foods and beverages:
- There are no restrictions, although Ceclor is more

CECLOR (continued)

effective if taken one hour before or two hours after a meal. Nevertheless, it can be taken at any time.

Other Medicines, Prescription or OTC:
• Ceclor interacts with other antibiotics. Tell your doctor if your child is taking any other drugs.

Other:
• If mild diarrhea is a side effect, ask your doctor if you can give your child yogurt. The beneficial bacteria in yogurt replace the intestine's natural beneficial bacteria that have been reduced or eliminated by Ceclor.

Medical Tests: Ceclor interferes with the results of some blood and urine tests, including tests for glucose.

CODEINE (GENERIC)

Ingredient(s): codeine

Equivalent Product(s): Codeine is available as a single drug in generic form only. However, many brand name combination products contain codeine.

Used For: relief of mild to moderate pain and for dry cough

Dosage Form and Strength: tablets—15 mg, 30 mg, 60 mg; soluble tablets—15 mg, 30 mg, 60 mg

Storage: Store in a dry, tightly closed container away from light.

Before Using This Medication Tell Your Doctor: if your child has a history of liver, kidney, heart, or thyroid conditions; a recent head injury; asthma; or epilepsy or other convulsive disorder. Also tell your doctor about any drugs, prescription or nonprescription, your child is taking and about any allergies your child has or any family history of allergies.

This Drug Should Not Be Used If: your child is allergic to it. This drug is not recommended for use with children under two years of age.

How to Use: Give this medication with food or milk to prevent stomach upset.

Time Required for Drug to Take Effect: fifteen to thirty minutes

Missing a Dose: Give the missed dose as soon as possible unless it is almost time for the next dose. In this case, do not give the missed dose, but return to the regular schedule. Never double the dose.

Symptoms of Overdose: severe drowsiness, nausea, vomiting, restlessness, excitability, deep sleep, convulsions,

CODEINE (GENERIC) (*continued*)

clammy skin, shallow breathing, constricted pupils, limpness

Side Effects:

Minor and expected:
• drowsiness, dry mouth, constipation, light-headedness

Serious adverse reactions (CALL YOUR DOCTOR):
• rash, hives, itching, nausea, vomiting, dizziness, sweating, headache, sleeplessness, mood changes, tremors, uncoordinated muscles

Effects of Long-Term Use: physical and psychological dependence

Habit-Forming Possibility: Strong. This drug can lead to dependence when used in large doses and/or for long periods of time.

Precautions and Suggestions:

Foods and beverages:
• There are no restrictions except that alcohol should be avoided. Even though your child does not drink alcoholic beverages, make sure that you are not giving another medication containing alcohol to your child.

Other Medicines, Prescription or OTC:
• Codeine interacts with other narcotics, sedatives, tranquilizers, painkillers, and antidepressants.
• Codeine interacts with the drug chlordiazepoxide (Librium).
• Aspirin and the antibiotic chloramphenicol increase the painkilling action of codeine.

Other:
• If this drug causes your child to become drowsy, do not allow him or her to engage in activities that require

CODEINE (GENERIC) (continued)

alertness—bike riding, skateboarding, swimming, or tree climbing.
- If it has been necessary to give this medication to your child for a long period of time, ask your doctor how to reduce the dosage and eventually stop giving the drug.

Medical Tests: no interactions

CORTISPORIN OPHTHALMIC

Ingredient(s): hydrocortisone, neomycin sulfate, polymyxin
   B sulfate, and (ointment only) bacitracin zinc

Equivalent Product(s): none

Used For: treatment of bacterial infection and inflammation
   of the eye

Dosage Form and Strength: suspension—1.0% hydrocortisone, 0.5% neomycin sulfate, and 10,000 units polymyxin B sulfate per ml; ointment—1.0% hydrocortisone,
   0.5% neomycin sulfate, 400 units bacitracin zinc, and
   10,000 units polymyxin B sulfate per gram

Storage: Store in tightly closed containers.

Before Using This Medication Tell Your Doctor: if your
   child has an eye condition in addition to the one for
   which he or she is now being treated; a viral or fungal
   infection, including chicken pox and herpes simplex (cold
   sore); kidney disease; inner ear disease; or tuberculosis.
   Tell your doctor about any drugs, prescription or nonprescription your child is taking or about any allergies your
   child has or any family history of allergies.

This Drug Should Not Be Used If: your child is allergic to
   any of its ingredients or has a fungal or viral disease of
   the eye, an inflammation of the cornea caused by herpes
   simplex virus, or chicken pox.

How to Use: See Chapter 8 for detailed instructions. The
   suspension form of this medicine must be shaken well
   before using.

Time Required for Drug to Take Effect: three to four days.

Missing a Dose: Give the missed dose as soon as you remember
   and then return to the regular schedule. If it is almost time

CORTISPORIN OPHTHALMIC

(*continued*)

for the next dose, however, skip the missed dose and continue to maintain the regular schedule. Do not double the dose.

Symptoms of Overdose: superinfection—a second infection in addition to the infection being treated. A superinfection is caused by bacteria and other organisms that are not susceptible to or affected by the drug being used to treat the original infection. Thus, these organisms, which are normally too few in number to cause problems, grow unchecked and cause a second infection that may require a different drug to treat.

Side Effects:

Minor and expected:
• temporary burning, itching, and blurring sensations when medication is first applied

Serious adverse reactions (CALL YOUR DOCTOR):
• swelling, eye pain, rash, persistent blurring, redness, decreased vision, severe eye irritation

Effects of Long-Term Use: superinfection—a second infection in addition to the infection being treated. A superinfection is caused by bacteria and other organisms that are not susceptible to or affected by the drug being used to treat the original infection. Thus, these organisms, which are normally too few in number to cause problems, grow unchecked and cause a second infection that may require a different drug to treat.

Habit-Forming Possibility: none

CORTISPORIN OPHTHALMIC

(*continued*)

Precautions and Suggestions:

Foods and beverages:
- no restrictions

Other Medicines, Prescription or OTC:
- This drug may interact with other antibiotics. Be sure to tell your doctor if your child is taking any other antibiotics.

Other:
- Continue to give this drug as long as your doctor specifies, even if the symptoms clear up.
- When treatment is completed, discard any leftover medicine.
- Do not use the medicine if it has changed in color.
- Do not allow your child to apply makeup to an infected eye.

Medical Tests: Your doctor may want to perform laboratory tests and eye examinations periodically, especially if the treatment is prolonged.

CORTISPORIN OTIC

Ingredient(s): hydrocortisone, neomycin sulfate, polymyxin B sulfate

Equivalent Product(s): none

Used For: treatment of bacterial infection and inflammation of the outer ear canal

Dosage Form and Strength: solution and suspension—1.0% hydrocortisone, 5 mg neomycin sulfate, and 10,000 units polymyxin B sulfate per ml

Storage: Store in a tightly closed container.

Before Using This Medication Tell Your Doctor: if your child has kidney disease or a fungal or viral skin condition. Tell the doctor if your child has had any ear problems besides the one being treated now. Tell your doctor about any drugs, prescription or OTC, your child is taking and about any allergies your child has or any family history of allergies.

This Drug Should Not Be Used If: your child is allergic to any of its ingredients or has a viral or fungal skin condition such as chicken pox or herpes simplex. This drug should not be used if the child's eardrum is perforated.

How to Use: Refer to Chapter 8 for detailed instructions.

Time Required for Drug to Take Effect: one to two days

Missing a Dose: Give the missed dose as soon as possible and then return to the regular schedule. If, however, it is almost time for the next dose, wait until the scheduled time. Do not double the dose.

Symptoms of Overdose: there are no data that overdose has occurred

CORTISPORIN OTIC (*continued*)

Side Effects:

   Minor and expected:
- burning or stinging sensation

   Serious adverse reactions (CALL YOUR DOCTOR):
- redness, swelling, itching, hives

Effects of Long-Term Use: Unknown. This drug should not be used for more than 10 days.

Habit-Forming Possibility: none

Precautions and Suggestions:

   Foods and beverages:
- no restrictions

   Other Medicines, Prescription or OTC:
- Be sure to tell your doctor if your child is taking any other antibiotics.

   Other:
- After completing the prescribed course of drug therapy, throw away any remaining medication so you won't be tempted to treat a future ear problem without consulting your doctor.
- Do not use the medication if its color or other characteristics have changed in any manner since you purchased it.
- Try not to miss any doses.

Medical Tests: no interactions

CROMOLYN SODIUM (GENERIC)

Ingredient(s): cromolyn sodium (disodium cromoglycate)

Equivalent Product(s): Intal, Nasalcrom

Used For: prevention of attacks of severe bronchial asthma and prevention and treatment of runny nose due to an allergy. This drug will not relieve an asthma attack once it has begun; cromolyn is strictly a preventive medication.

Dosage Form and Strength: capsules for inhalation only—20 mg; solution for spray device—20 mg per 2 ml ampule; nasal solution—40 mg per ml. Each spray delivers 5.2 mg.

Storage: Store in a dry, tightly closed container in a cool, dark place. Do not refrigerate. Do not handle the inhaler or capsules with wet hands.

Before Using This Medication Tell Your Doctor: if your child has a history of liver or kidney disease. Also tell your doctor about any drugs, prescription or nonprescription, that your child is taking (especially other drugs for asthma) and about any allergies your child has or any family history of allergies.

This Drug Should Not Be Used If: your child has an allergy to its ingredient. Because the capsule may be difficult to inhale, its use is not recommended for children under the age of five years. The safety and effectiveness of the nasal solution have not been established for children under the age of six years. Likewise, the safety and effectiveness of the spray solution have not been established for children younger than two years.

How to Use: The capsules are to be inhaled, not taken by mouth. Ask your doctor to explain and demonstrate how

CROMOLYN SODIUM (GENERIC) (*continued*)

to inhale the capsules. Also, ask your pharmacist to include a sheet of patient instructions with the prescription. Be certain you understand how to use this form of the medication before you give it to your child. The spray solution should be administered from a power-operated sprayer equipped with a face mask. A hand-operated sprayer is not acceptable. The spray should also be inhaled. Ask your doctor to show you and the child how to use this product. After using both the capsules and spray inhaler, have your child rinse his or her mouth and throat with water to prevent irritation. The nasal solution should be sprayed once into each nostril at regular intervals during the day. The child should clear out his or her nose before using the spray and should inhale through the nose while spraying the solution. This solution should be administered with a metered spray device that should be replaced every six months. Ask your doctor to explain how to use this product.

Time Required for Drug to Take Effect: two to four weeks

Missing a Dose: Try not to miss a dose; this medication is effective only if taken at regular intervals. If you do forget, give the missed dose immediately. If it is almost time for the next dose, space that next dose midway through the regular intervals between doses. For example, if you are to give a dose at 8:00, 12:00, 4:00, and 8:00 and you remember at 7:00 P.M. that you forgot the 4:00 P.M. dose, give the missed dose at 7:00 P.M. but wait until about 9:30 or 10:00 P.M. to give the 8:00 P.M. dose. Then return to your regular schedule. Do not skip a dose or double the dose.

CROMOLYN SODIUM (GENERIC) *(continued)*

Symptoms of Overdose: none reported

Side Effects:

Minor and expected:
- mild cough, throat irritation, or hoarseness; sneezing; nasal burning and stinging

Serious adverse reactions (CALL YOUR DOCTOR):
- rash, spasm of bronchial tubes with shortness of breath, severe cough, nosebleed, adominal pain, nausea, headache, drowsiness, dizziness, pain and swelling in joints, difficult urination

Effects of Long-Term Use: allergic reaction of lung tissue leading to a condition resembling pneumonia

Habit-Forming Possibility: none

Precautions and Suggestions:

Foods and beverages:
- There are no specific restrictions except to avoid foods to which your child is allergic.

Other Medicines, Prescription or OTC:
- Cromolyn may interact with the bronchodilator isoproterenol. Tell your doctor if your child is using a bronchodilator.
- The use of cromolyn may make it possible to reduce or discontinue cortisone or steroid drugs your child may be taking for asthma. Do not adjust the doses yourself, but discuss this with your doctor.

Other:
- Do not stop giving cromolyn abruptly; this may trigger a return of an asthma attack.

CROMOLYN SODIUM (GENERIC) (*continued*)

- Do not allow the capsule to be swallowed. If your child does swallow the capsule accidentally, there will be no ill effects, but there will also be no beneficial effects.
- Do not change recommended dosages yourself. Sometimes cromolyn is effective enough that a parent believes the dosage can be reduced. This may trigger an asthma attack. Always talk with your doctor before changing a drug's dosage.

Medical Tests: Your doctor may suggest tests to examine your child's lungs if he or she develops symptoms suggesting an allergic reaction of lung tissue to the drug.

DILANTIN

Ingredient(s): phenytoin

Equivalent Product(s): none

Used For: control of epileptic seizures

Dosage Form and Strength: chewable tablets (Infatab)—50 mg; oral suspension—30 mg and 125 mg per 5 ml

Storage: Store at room temperature.

Before Using This Medication Tell Your Doctor: if your child has a history of liver, kidney, or heart disease; diabetes; low blood pressure; or bone disorders. Also tell your doctor about any medications, OTC or prescription, your child is taking; this includes aspirin and aspirin products, antibiotics, sulfa drugs, antacids, steroid drugs, some antidepressants, and other anticonvulsants. Be certain to tell your doctor about any allergies your child has.

This Drug Should Not Be Used If: your child is allergic to its ingredient.

How to Use: Give this drug with food to minimize stomach upset and to improve absorption. Shake the oral suspension well and measure in a medical teaspoon or dropper.

Time Required for Drug to Take Effect: It generally takes one to two weeks for the blood levels to stabilize.

Missing a Dose: Give the missed dose as soon as you remember unless it is almost time for the next dose, in which case eliminate the missed dose and return to the regular dosing schedule. Do not double the next dose. *Call your doctor if your child has a seizure as a result of missing a dose.*

DILANTIN (*continued*)

Symptoms of Overdose: constant involuntary movements of the eyeball, muscular incoordination, difficulty in moving joints, loss of consciousness

Side Effects:

Minor and expected:
- nausea, vomiting, diarrhea, constipation, drowsiness, dizziness, nervousness, insomnia, fatigue, irritability, headache, muscle twitching, tender gums, reddish or light brown urine, blurred vision

Serious adverse reactions (CALL YOUR DOCTOR):
- rash, swollen glands, severe nausea or vomiting, joint pain, yellow discoloration of the skin, bleeding gums, sore throat, unexplained fever, unusual bleeding or bruising, persistent headache, chest pain, confusion, slurred speech, mouth sores

Effects of Long-Term Use: disorders of immune system, malignancies

Habit-Forming Possibility: none

Precautions and Suggestions:

Foods and beverages:
- no restrictions

Other Medicines, Prescription or OTC:
- This drug may interact with aspirin, aspirin products, some antibiotics, sulfa drugs, antacids, antidepressants, steroid drugs, and other anticonvulsants.

Other:
- Do not discontinue medication or change dosage without talking with your doctor.

DILANTIN (*continued*)

- To prevent overgrowth of gum tissue, have your child maintain good oral hygiene, including flossing and gum massage.
- If this drug causes drowsiness, be certain that your child is careful when riding a bike, climbing a tree, or engaging in other activities that require alertness.
- There are other drugs that contain phenytoin, but they are not equivalent to Dilantin. Do not switch brands or request a generic drug without talking to your doctor.
- Phenobarbital is prescribed more often for epilepsy.
- Your child should carry an identification card stating that he or she has epilepsy and is taking Dilantin.

Medical Tests: Your doctor may want to perform periodic lab tests to monitor your child's progress while taking this drug. Dilantin may affect the results of blood and urine tests. Usage is monitored by measuring blood levels.

DIMETAPP

Ingredient(s): phenylpropanolamine, phenylephrine hydrochloride, brompheniramine

Equivalent Product(s): Bromalix, Bromophen, Dimalix, Dimaphen, E-Tapp, Histatapp, Midatap, Normatane, Purebrom, S-T Decongest SF and DF, Tagatap, Tamine, Tri-Phen, Veltap

Used For: relief of allergy symptoms and respiratory congestion

Dosage Form and Strength: elixir—5 mg phenylpropanolamine, 5 mg phenylephrine hydrochloride, 4 mg brompheniramine per 5 ml

Storage: Store at room temperature.

Before Using This Medication Tell Your Doctor: if your child has a history of asthma, high blood pressure, heart disease, circulatory disease, diabetes, ulcers, thyroid problems, seizures, or urinary tract obstruction. Also tell your doctor about any drug, prescription or nonprescription, your child is using and about any allergies your child has or any family history of allergies.

This Drug Should Not Be Used If: your child is allergic to its ingredients; has high blood pressure, a heart condition, an obstructed bladder; or is taking certain antidepressants. This drug should not be used to treat asthma. This drug should be used cautiously for young children.

How to Use: Give the medication with a glass of water or with food or milk. Measure the dose in a medical teaspoon.

Time Required for Drug to Take Effect: approximately 30 minutes to one hour

Missing a Dose: Give the missed dose as soon as you remember. However, if it is almost time for the next dose, do

DIMETAPP (*continued*)

not give the missed dose; return to the regular schedule. Do not double the next dose.

Symptoms of Overdose: excitement, clumsiness, muscle spasms, hallucinations, convulsions, dilated pupils, flushed face, fever, shallow breathing, weak and rapid pulse, headache, sweating, nausea, vomiting

Side Effects:

Minor and expected:
- drowsiness, thickening of lung and respiratory secretions, nausea, vomiting, diarrhea, constipation, dizziness, nervousness, restless sleeping, headache, dry mouth, loss of appetite

Serious adverse reactions (CALL YOUR DOCTOR):
- vision disturbances, skin rashes, hives, tight chest, unusual bleeding or bruising, fast or pounding heartbeat, chest pain, unexplained sore throat and fever, clumsiness, unusual weakness, ringing in the ears, difficult or painful urination

Effects of Long-Term Use: This type of medication should not be used for a prolonged period of time. If it is used too long, it may produce involuntary movements of lips, tongue, and jaw; possible reduction in the ability of the bone marrow, the soft connective tissue inside the bones, to do its job of manufacturing blood cells; and worsening of congestion rather than relief.

Habit-Forming Possibility: none, unless it is used so frequently or so long that the body becomes dependent on the drug to perform the functions the body would normally do

DIMETAPP (*continued*)

Precautions and Suggestions:

Foods and beverage: no restrictions

Other Medicines, Prescription or OTC:
- This drug may interact with other antihistamines, anti-depressants, medications for coughs and colds, asthma and breathing medicines, narcotics, painkillers, seizure medicine, sedatives, and tranquilizers.

Other:
- If this drug causes your child to become drowsy, do not allow him or her to engage in activities that require alertness, such as bike riding, skateboarding, swimming, or tree climbing.
- Call your doctor if this drug causes excited or over-stimulated behavior in your child.

Medical Tests: Your doctor may want to take blood cell counts while this medication is being used.

ERYTHROMYCIN (GENERIC)

Ingredient(s): erythromycin

Equivalent Product(s): Bristamycin, E.E.S., E-Mycin, Eramycin, Eryc, Erypar, EryPed, Ery-Tab, Erythrocin, Ethril, Ilosone, Pediamycin, Pfizer-E, SK-Erythromycin, Wyamycin

Used For: a wide variety of bacterial infections

Dosage Form and Strength: tablets (includes chewable and enteric or film-coated), capsules, drops, and oral suspension—various strengths

Storage: Store liquid forms of this drug in the refrigerator. Store other forms in tightly closed containers at room temperature.

Before Using This Medication Tell Your Doctor: if your child has a history of bronchial asthma, sensitivity to aspirin, or liver disease. Also tell your doctor about any drugs, prescription or nonprescription, that your child is using (especially bronchodilators, anticonvulsants, and other antibiotics) and about any known allergies or family history of allergies.

This Drug Should Not Be Used If: your child is allergic to erythromycin or has liver disease.

How to Use: This drug should preferably be given on an empty stomach, one hour before or two hours after a meal. However, if stomach upset occurs, you can give this drug with food. Some types of erythromycin can be taken without regard to food or meals. Ask your doctor which type is being prescribed for your child. If you are using the oral suspension, shake the bottle well and measure the dose with a medical teaspoon. If you are giving drops to a baby, measure the medicine in a

ERYTHROMYCIN (GENERIC)

(*continued*)

marked dropper and release the liquid into the inside of the child's cheek. Have the child take each dose with at least one half to one full glass of water. Give the medication at evenly spaced intervals, preferably around the clock. Give the full amount of medication until it is gone, even if your child seems and feels well.

Time Required for Drug to Take Effect: varies, depending on the illness being treated

Missing a Dose: Give the missed dosed immediately. If you did not remember to give the missed dose until almost time for the next dose, space that next dose about midway through the normal interval between doses. For example, if you are to give a dose at 8:00, 12:00, 4:00 and 8:00 and you remember at 7:00 P.M. that you forgot the 4:00 P.M. dose, give the missed dose at 7:00 P.M. but wait until 10:00 P.M. to give the 8:00 P.M. dose. Then return to your normal schedule. Do not skip a dose or double the dose.

Symptoms of Overdose: severe nausea, vomiting, abdominal discomfort, diarrhea

Side Effects:

Minor and expected:
• nausea, vomiting, diarrhea, stomach cramps

Serious adverse reactions (CALL YOUR DOCTOR):
• severe abdominal pain, yellow discoloration of skin or eyes, dark urine, pale-colored stools, unusual fatigue, hearing loss, rash, itching, superinfection

Effects of Long-Term Use: superinfection—a second infection in addition to the infection being treated. The superinfection is caused by bacteria and other organisms

ERYTHROMYCIN (GENERIC)

(*continued*)

that are not susceptible to or affected by the drug being used to treat the original infection. Thus, these organisms, which normally are too few in number to cause problems, grow unchecked and cause a second infection that may require a different drug to treat.

Habit-Forming Possibility: none

Precautions and Suggestions:

Foods and beverages:
• no restrictions

Other Medicines, Prescription or OTC:
• Erythromycin may affect the effects of theophylline or carbamazepine in the body. Be sure to tell your doctor if your child is taking theophylline for asthma or breathing problems or carbamazepine for epilepsy.
• Some of the forms of erythromycin contain a dye called *tartrazine*, which may cause allergic-type reactions (including bronchial asthma) in some people, especially those sensitive to aspirin.

Other:
• If mild diarrhea is a side effect, ask your doctor if you can give your child yogurt. The beneficial bacteria in yogurt replace the intestine's natural beneficial bacteria that have been reduced or eliminated by erythromycin.
• Do not use the medication beyond the expiration date on the container.

Medical Tests: Erythromycin interferes with urine laboratory tests.

GANTRISIN

Ingredient(s): sulfisoxazole

Equivalent Product(s): SK-Soxazole, sulfisoxazole (generic), Sulfizin

Used For: treatment of a variety of bacterial infections, especially in the urinary tract

Dosage Form and Strength: tablets—500 mg; syrup—500 mg per 5 ml teaspoon; pediatric suspension—500 mg per 5 ml teaspoon

Storage: Store in a tightly closed container at room temperature.

Before Using This Medication Tell Your Doctor: if your child has any kidney or liver disorders, an obstruction in the urinary or intestinal tract, strep throat,, a history of allergies or bronchial asthma, or glucose-6-phosphate dehydrogenase deficiency. Also, tell your doctor about any drugs, prescription or nonprescription, that your child is using and about any allergies your child has or any family history of allergies.

This Drug Should Not Be Used If: your child is allergic to its ingredient or to any sulfa drugs. This drug should not be used if the child has a urinary or intestinal obstruction or if the child has a strep throat. This drug is not recommended for children under two months of age.

How to Use: This drug should be given on an empty stomach at least one hour before or two hours after meals with a full glass of water. However, if stomach upset occurs, you can give this drug with food. Encourage the child to drink as much water as possible during the day—preferably eight glasses. If you are using the liquid versions of this drug, shake the bottle thoroughly and measure with a medical teaspoon. Give the medicine at evenly spaced

GANTRISIN (*continued*)

intervals around the clock. Give the full amount of medication until it is gone, even if the child seems and feels well.

Time Required for Drug to Take Effect: varies, depending on the illness being treated, usually two to five days

Missing a Dose: Give the missed dose as soon as you remember, unless it is almost time for the next dose. In that case, if your child is taking three or more doses a day, space the missed dose and the next dose two to four hours apart. Then return to your regular dosing schedule.

Symptoms of Overdose: severe nausea, vomiting, dizziness, headache, drowsiness, yellowing of skin and eyes, and loss of consciousness

Side Effects:

Minor and expected:
- loss of appetite, nausea, vomiting, depression, headache, dizziness, sleeplessness, and sensitivity to sunlight. This drug will also cause a brown discoloration of the urine, which is harmless.

Serious adverse reactions (CALL YOUR DOCTOR):
- unexplained sore throat or fever, paleness, purplish or yellowish discoloration of the skin, rash, itching, abdominal pains, bloody diarrhea, difficulty in urination, unusual bleeding or bruising, pain in muscles and joints, breathing or swallowing difficulties, hearing loss, ringing in the ears, loss of coordination, hair loss, blood in urine, chills, swelling of the face or neck, mouth sores

Effects of Long-Term Use: superinfection—a second infection in addition to the infection being treated. A

GANTRISIN (continued)

superinfection is caused by bacteria and other organisms that are not susceptible to or affected by the drug being used to treat the original infection. Thus, these organisms, which are normally too few in number to cause problems, grow unchecked and cause a second infection that may require a different drug to treat. Also, possible enlargement of the thyroid gland with or without impaired functioning of the gland.

Habit-Forming Possibility: none

Precautions and Suggestions:

Foods and beverages:
• No restrictions

Other Medicines, Prescription or OTC:
• Gantrisin may interact with aspirin-type drugs (salicylates), the anticonvulsant phenytoin, methenamines, local anesthetics, and para-aminobenzoic acid (PABA) found in some sunscreens. It also interacts with some oral diabetes drugs.

Other:
• If this drug causes your child to become increasingly sensitive to the sun, be certain that he or she is protected from exposure to the sun, but do not use a sunscreen with PABA in it.
• If this drug causes drowsiness or dizziness, do not allow your child to engage in activities requiring alertness, such as bicycling, skateboarding, tree climbing, and swimming.

Medical Tests: Your doctor may want to perform blood tests to monitor your child's progress while taking this drug. Gantrisin can interfere with the results of urine tests for glucose (sugar) and protein.

KENALOG

Ingredient(s): triamcinolone acetonide

Equivalent Product(s): Aristocort, Flutex, Kenac, triamcinolone acetonide (generic), Trymex

Used For: relief of skin inflammation, swelling, and itching symptoms caused by skin diseases

Dosage Form and Strength: ointment—0.025%, 0.1%, 0.5%; cream—0.025%, 0.1%, 0.5%; lotion—0.025%, 0.1%; aerosol—two-second spray delivers about 0.2 mg

Storage: Store away from light in a tightly closed container.

Before Using This Medication Tell Your Doctor: if your child has a fungus infection or any other infection, tuberculosis of the skin, chicken pox, shingles, herpes simplex on the skin, a perforated eardrum, diabetes, ulcer, or a circulatory system disorder. Also tell your doctor about any drugs, prescription or nonprescription, your child is using and about any allergies your child has or any family history of allergies.

This Drug Should Not Be Used If: your child is allergic to its contents or to any steroid drugs or has a fungal infection, any other infection, tuberculosis of the skin, chicken pox, shingles, herpes simplex, or a perforated eardrum. It should not be used for children under two years of age.

How to Use: First wash your hands and then gently wash the affected area of skin with water; pat dry. Apply the medication in a thin film; rub in lightly. Do not apply a thick layer. Do not bandage or wrap the area unless the doctor tells you to do so and shows you how. Shake the lotion well. If you are using the aerosol, do not breathe the vapors and do not pierce, puncture, or burn the can. *Do not allow the medication to get into the child's eyes.*

KENALOG (continued)

Time Required for Drug to Take Effect: Benefits may be apparent in 24 to 48 hours. The dosage may then have to be adjusted to provide maximum benefit; this usually occurs in four to ten days. It is important to adjust the dosage so that the smallest possible dose that will still achieve the desired effect is given.

Missing a Dose: Apply the missed dose as soon as you remember. However, if it is almost time for the next dose, do not apply the missed dose, but return to the original schedule. Do not place twice as much medication on the skin at the next dose.

Symptoms of Overdose: fatigue, increased sweating, muscle weakness, indigestion, muscle cramping, flushed face, behavior changes

Side Effects:

Minor and expected:
- a stinging or burning sensation may occur when the medicine is applied; this is harmless.

Serious adverse reactions (CALL YOUR DOCTOR):
- severe burning or stinging; itching, blistering, peeling, or any signs of irritation that were not present when you started to use Kenalog; increased hair growth; thinning of the skin; loss of skin color; signs of infection on the skin; purplish discoloration of the skin; abnormal lines on the skin; increased sweating; muscle weakness and cramping; flushed face; indigestion; fatigue; behavior changes

Effects of Long-Term Use: slowing of growth and development in children, weight gain, thinning of skin, easy bruising, loss of bone strength, increase in blood sugar (possibly leading to diabetes), eye problems.

KENALOG (*continued*)

Habit-Forming Possibility: possible functional dependence, in which a body function becomes dependent on the drug to do the job of the function

Precautions and Suggestions:

Foods and beverages:
- no restrictions

Other Medicines, Prescription or OTC:
- Do not use this medication at the same time as you are using another steroid medication. Young children can absorb a great deal of the steroid drug in this topical medication; therefore, using still another steroid medicine, oral or topical, at the same time can lead to an overdose.
- Kenalog may interact with barbiturates, sedatives, aspirin, phenytoin, antihistamines, and antidiabetic drugs.
- This drug may decrease the effects of insulin in diabetic children.
- Do not allow your child to receive a vaccination while you are using this medicine.

Other:
- If your child is treated by any other doctor or dentist while you are using Kenalog, be certain to tell that medical care provider that your child is using this medication.
- If you are applying Kenalog in your child's diaper area, do not use tight-fitting diapers or plastic pants.

Medical Tests: Your doctor may recommend tests to monitor your child's progress.

LINDANE (GENERIC)

Ingredient(s): gamma benzene hexachloride

Equivalent Product(s): Kwell, Scabene

Used For: treatment of head and crab lice and their eggs. Cream and lotion forms also are used to treat scabies.

Dosage Form and Strength: cream—1%; lotion—1%; shampoo—1%

Storage: Store all forms of this product at room temperature.

Before Using This Medication Tell Your Doctor: if your child has any allergies. Also tell your doctor about any medication, prescription or nonprescription, your child is taking.

This Drug Should Not Be Used If: your child is allergic to its ingredient.

How to Use: When using cream or lotion to treat for lice, apply enough to cover thinly the entire affected area. Rub the medicine into the skin and hair and leave it on for eight to 12 hours. Then wash thoroughly. You usually will not have to apply a second treatment unless you see living lice after seven days. When using shampoo, apply two tablespoons of shampoo to your child's dry hair. Add small quantities of water and work into hair and skin until good lather forms. Do not allow shampoo to get into your child's eyes or mouth. Continue shampooing for four minutes. Rinse the hair well with water. Towel and comb with a fine-tooth comb to remove the nits (eggs). You should not have to repeat the treatment unless you find living lice seven days later. Do not use the shampoo more than two times. Do not use it as a routine shampoo. For scabies, apply a thin coating of the cream or lotion to dry skin all over your child's body

LINDANE (GENERIC) (continued)

from the neck down. Rub it in thoroughly. Leave it on for eight to 12 hours and then remove the medicine by washing thoroughly. One application is usually all that is needed.

Time Required for Drug to Take Effect: shampoo—four minutes; cream and lotion—eight to 12 hours.

Missing a Dose: not applicable

Symptoms of Overdose: This product can penetrate the skin and have an effect on the central nervous system. There have been reports of seizures following the use of this drug, but it has not been definitely proved that the drug was the cause. Studies have shown that potential adverse effects of this medication are greater in young children. Discuss the use of this drug with your doctor.

Side Effects:

Minor and expected:
• none

Serious adverse reactions (CALL YOUR DOCTOR):
• possible seizures, skin rash, itching, burning

Effects of Long-Term Use: not applicable

Habit-Forming Possibility: not applicable

Precautions and Suggestions:

Foods and beverages:
• not applicable

Other Medicines, Prescription or OTC:
• no restrictions

Other:
• Do not apply to the face and avoid getting the product in the eyes.

LINDANE (GENERIC) (*continued*)

- Do not use more than the amount prescribed.
- This medication is poisonous if swallowed or absorbed through the skin; make sure you rinse it off thoroughly after the prescribed treatment time. Keep this medication out of the reach of children.
- If one person within your household has lice, all family members except pregnant women and infants should be treated for lice.
- After shampooing and rinsing the hair, sometimes an additional vinegar rinse will loosen the nits (eggs) so that you can comb them out.
- Be certain to clean hairbrushes and combs with lindane and to launder hats, clothing, and bedding thoroughly

Medical Tests: not applicable

MYCOSTATIN

Ingredient(s): nystatin

Equivalent Product(s): nystatin (generic), Nilstat

Used For: treatment of yeast and fungal infections

Dosage Form and Strength: tablets—500,000 units; oral suspension—100,000 units per ml; cream or ointment—100,000 units per gram

Storage: Store at room temperature.

Before Using This Medication Tell Your Doctor: about any drug, prescription or nonprescription, your child is taking and about any known allergies or family history of allergies.

This Drug Should Not Be Used If: your child is allergic to the ingredient in the drug.

How to Use: Give tablets as directed. Continue giving tablets for at least 48 hours after the infection clears up. Apply cream or ointment to affected areas after cleansing the areas unless instructed otherwise by your doctor. Continue using for one week after the infection has disappeared. If you are treating an infection in the mouth, have the child hold the oral suspension in his or her mouth and rinse it around as long as possible before swallowing. Shake the container well before using. Continue giving the medicine for at least 48 hours after the infection is gone.

Time Required for Drug to Take Effect: varies, depending on infection

Missing a Dose: Give the dose when you remember and then return to the regular dosing schedule. If you remember just before the next dose is due, wait until that time, give the dose, and simply continue the regular schedule.

MYCOSTATIN *(continued)*

Symptoms of Overdose: There is little possibility of overdosing, but nausea, vomiting, stomachache, and diarrhea have occurred in those taking large doses.

Side Effects:

Minor and expected:
• none

Serious adverse reactions (CALL YOUR DOCTOR):
• Nausea, vomiting, stomachache, diarrhea, skin irritation (ointment or cream)

Effects of Long-Term Use: none

Habit-Forming Possibility: none

Precautions and Suggestions:

Foods and beverages:
• no restrictions

Other Medicines, Prescription or OTC:
• no interactions

Other:
• The powder form is best used on wet, weeping sores.
• The oral suspension does not have to be refrigerated.
• Always complete the full course of medication, even if child seems well.

Medical Tests: no interactions

PEDIAZOLE

Ingredient(s): erythromycin ethylsuccinate and sulfisoxazole

Equivalent Product(s): none

Used For: treating acute middle ear infection caused by bacteria called *Hemophilus influenzae*

Dosage Form and Strength: oral suspension—200 mg erythromycin and 600 mg sulfisoxazole per 5 ml teaspoon

Storage: Store in the refrigerator. Use within 14 days and discard any unused portion after that time.

Before Using This Medication Tell Your Doctor: if your child has any kidney or liver disorders, an obstruction in the urinary or intestinal tract, a history of allergies or bronchial asthma, sensitivity to aspirin, or G6PD deficiency. Also tell your doctor about any drugs, prescription or nonprescription, that your child is using (especially bronchodilators, anticonvulsants, and other antibiotics) and about any allergies your child has or any family history of allergies.

This Drug Should Not Be Used If: your child is allergic to its ingredients or to any sulfa drugs. This drug should not be used by a child who has liver disease, a urinary or intestinal obstruction, or a strep throat. This drug is not to be given to children under two months of age.

How to Use: This drug can be given with or without food with a full glass of water. If stomach upset occurs, give the medicine with food. Encourage the child to drink as much water as possible during the day—preferably eight glasses. Shake the medicine container thoroughly and measure with a medical teaspoon. Give the medicine at evenly spaced intervals around the clock. Give the full amount until the medicine is gone, even if the child seems and feels well.

PEDIAZOLE (*continued*)

Time Required for Drug to Take Effect: varies, depending on the illness being treated, usually two to five days

Missing a Dose: Give the missed dose immediately. If you did not remember to give the missed dose until almost time for the next dose, space that dose about midway through the normal interval between doses. For example, if you are to give a dose at 8:00, 2:00, and 8:00 and you remember at 7:00 P.M. that you forgot the 4:00 P.M. dose, give the missed dose at 7:00 P.M. but wait until 11:00 P.M. to give the 8:00 P.M. dose. Then return to your normal schedule. Do not skip a dose or double the dose.

Symptoms of Overdose: severe nausea, vomiting, diarrhea, abdominal discomfort, dizziness, headache, drowsiness, yellowing of skin and eyes, loss of consciousness

Side Effects:

Minor and expected:
• loss of appetite, nausea, vomiting, diarrhea, stomach cramps, depression, headache, dizziness, sleeplessness, and sensitivity to sunlight. This drug may also cause a brown discoloration of the urine, which is harmless.

Serious adverse reactions (CALL YOUR DOCTOR):
• unexplained sore throat and fever, paleness, purplish or yellowish discoloration of skin, rash, itching, abdominal pains, bloody diarrhea, difficulty in urination, dark urine, pale-colored stools, unusual fatigue, unusual bleeding or bruising, pain in muscles and joints, breathing or swallowing difficulties, hearing loss, ringing in the ears, loss of coordination, hair loss, blood in urine, chills, swelling of face or neck, mouth sores

PEDIAZOLE (*continued*)

Effects of Long-Term Use: superinfection—a second infection in addition to the infection being treated. A superinfection is caused by bacteria and other organisms that are not susceptible to or affected by the drug being used to treat the original infection. Thus these organisms, which are normally too few in number to cause problems, grow unchecked and cause a second infection that may require a different drug to treat. Also, possible enlargement of thyroid gland with or without impaired functioning of the gland.

Habit-Forming Possibility: none

Precautions and Suggestions:

Foods and beverages:
- no restrictions

Other Medicines, Prescription or OTC:
- This drug may interact with aspirinlike drugs (salicylates), the anticonvulsant phenytoin, methenamines, local anesthetics, and para-aminobenzoic acid (PABA) found in some sunscreens. It may also interact with some oral diabetes drugs.
- This drug may also affect the effects of theophylline or carbamazepine in the body. Be sure to tell your doctor if your child is taking theophylline for asthma or breathing problems or carbamazepine for epilepsy.

Other:
- If this drug causes your child to become sensitive to the sun, be certain that he or she is protected from the sun, but do not use a sunscreen with PABA in it.
- If this drug causes your child to become drowsy or dizzy, do not allow him or her to engage in activities that require alertness, such as bike riding, skateboarding, swimming, or tree climbing.

PEDIAZOLE (*continued*)

- If mild diarrhea is a side effect, ask your doctor if you can give your child yogurt. The beneficial bacteria in yogurt replace the intestine's natural beneficial bacteria that have been reduced or eliminated by this drug.
- Do not use the medication beyond the expiration date on the container.

Medical Tests: Your doctor may want to perform blood tests to monitor your child's progress on this drug. This drug may affect the results of urine tests.

PENICILLIN V (GENERIC)

Ingredient(s): penicillin V

Equivalent Product(s): various and numerous generic equivalents

Used For: treating bacterial infections, including infections of the middle ear, respiratory tract, skin, and gums

Dosage Form and Strength: tablets—125 mg, 250 mg, 500 mg; oral solution—125 mg per 5 ml, 250 mg per 5 ml

Storage: Store the oral solution in the refrigerator and use it within 14 days; discard any unused portion after that time. Store the tablets in a tightly closed, light-resistant container in a cool place (below 85°F).

Before Using This Medication Tell Your Doctor: if your child has ever had an allergic or asthmatic reaction to a penicillin drug or any other antibiotics. Also tell your doctor if your child is allergic by nature or has ever had hay fever, hives, skin rashes, or any other allergic reactions to anything. Inform your doctor if your child has ever been diagnosed as having liver or kidney problems. Be sure to tell your doctor about any drugs, prescription or nonprescription, your child is using.

This Drug Should Not Be Used If: your child is allergic to penicillin or has previously had an allergic reaction to any form of penicillin.

How to Use: Give the medicine as directed by your doctor, usually at evenly spaced intervals around the clock. The drug can be taken with or without food. If you are using the oral solution, shake the container thoroughly and measure with a medical teaspoon. Give each dose with a full glass of water, not fruit juice or carbonated beverage. The oral solution and the tablets (crushed) can be

PENICILLIN V (GENERIC) (*continued*)

mixed with formula, milk, or water and given immediately. If you do this, you must be certain the child swallows the entire drink to receive the full dose of medicine. Give the full amount of medication until it is gone, even if the child seems and feels well.

Time Required for Drug to Take Effect: varies; depending on the illness being treated, usually two to five days

Missing a Dose: Give the missed dose immediately. If it is almost time for the next dose, wait to give the next dose until about halfway through the regular interval between doses. For example, if you are to give a dose at 8:00, 2:00 and 8:00 and you remember at 7:00 P.M. that you forgot the 2:00 P.M. dose, give the missed dose at 7:00 P.M. but wait until about 11:00 P.M. to give the 8:00 P.M. dose. Then return to your regular schedule. Do not skip a dose or double the dose.

Symptoms of Overdose: possible severe and persistent nausea, vomiting, and/or diarrhea

Side Effects:

Minor and expected:
• diarrhea, nausea

Serious adverse reactions (CALL YOUR DOCTOR):
• hives, itching, or skin rash; difficult breathing; fever; joint pain; sore throat; dark-colored tongue; yellow-green stools; sores in the mouth; severe and persistent nausea, vomiting, or diarrhea; unusual fatigue; confusion; depression; convulsions

Effects of Long-Term Use: superinfection—a second infection in addition to the infection being treated. A superinfection is caused by bacteria and other organisms

PENICILLIN V (GENERIC) (*continued*)

that are not susceptible to or affected by the drug being used to treat the original infection. Thus, these organisms, which are normally too few in number to cause problems, grow unchecked and cause a second infection that may require a different drug to treat.

Habit-Forming Possibility: none

Precautions and Suggestions:

Foods and beverages:
- no restrictions

Other Medicines, Prescription or OTC:
- Pencillin V may interact with other antibiotics, particularly erythromycin and tetracyline, and with neomycin. Penicillin may also decrease the effectiveness of oral contraceptives.

Other:
- If mild diarrhea is a side effect, ask your doctor if you can give your child yogurt. The beneficial bacteria in yogurt replace the intestine's natural beneficial bacteria that have been reduced or eliminated by the penicillin.
- Do not use this drug beyond the expiration date on the label.

Medical Tests: Your doctor may recommend blood tests and liver and kidney function tests during treatment with this drug in order to monitor your child's progress.
- This drug may affect the results of laboratory tests.

PHENOBARBITAL (GENERIC)

Ingredient(s): phenobarbital

Equivalent Product(s): Barbita, Luminal Ovoids, PBR/12, Sedadrops, SK-Phenobarbital, Solfoton

Used For: control of convulsions or seizures, relief of anxiety or tension, and as a sleeping aid

Dosage Form and Strength: tablets—8 mg, 15 mg, 16 mg, 30 mg, 32 mg, 65 mg, 100 mg; capsules—16 mg; timed-released capsules—65 mg; drops—16 mg per ml; liquid—15 mg per 5 ml; elixir—20 mg per 5 ml

Storage: Store capsules and tablets in dry, tightly closed container at room temperature. Store liquid in tightly closed, dark-colored container.

Before Using This Medication Tell Your Doctor: if your child has chronic lung disease, diabetes, epilepsy, liver of kidney disease, overactive thyroid, anemia, porphyria (an inherited disease characterized by liver involvement and sensitivity to sunlight), or a history of hyperactivity. Also tell your doctor about any drugs, prescription or nonprescription, your child is using and about any allergies your child has or any family history of allergy.

This Drug Should Not Be Used If: your child is allergic to its ingredient or to any barbiturate or if your child has liver or kidney disease, respiratory disease, or porphyria.

How to Use: Give phenobarbital with food or a full glass of water. Measure the liquid forms with a medical teaspoon. You can also crush the tablets or open the regular capsules and place the drug in food, but the child must eat all the food in order to receive the full dose. You must not open the timed-release capsule; it must be swallowed whole.

PHENOBARBITAL (GENERIC)

(*continued*)

Time Required for Drug to Take Effect: about one hour

Missing a Dose: If you remember within an hour of the regular dosage time, give the missed dose and then return to the regular dosing schedule. If more than an hour has passed, do not give the missed dose; instead return to the regular schedule. Do not double the next dose.

Symptoms of Overdose: confusion, slurred speech, drowsiness, clumsiness, staggering walk, slow and shallow breathing, weak and rapid pulse, cold and sweaty skin, deep sleep, eventual coma

Side Effects:

Minor and expected:
• drowsiness, sleepiness, a hangover-type feeling, dizziness, nausea, vomiting, diarrhea, headache, muscle pain, joint pain

Serious adverse reactions (CALL YOUR DOCTOR):
• sore throat, fever, easy bruising, nosebleed, purplish spots on skin, skin rash, hives, swelling around the face, difficult breathing, wheezing, tightness in the chest, slow heartbeat, fatigue, extreme sleepiness during the day, yellowish discoloration of the skin and eyes, depression, slurred speech, confusion, unsteadiness, unusual nervousness or excitement, nightmares, hallucinations, sleeplessness

Effects of Long-Term Use: anemia, dependence

Habit-Forming Possibility: This drug can lead to both physical and psychological dependence. This drug has potential for abuse since tolerance to it can develop easily.

PHENOBARBITAL (GENERIC)

(*continued*)

Precautions and Suggestions:

Foods and beverages:
- no restrictions

Other Medicines, Prescription or OTC:
- Phenobarbital may interact with anticonvulsants, central nervous system depressants (sedatives, sleeping aids, antihistamines, tranquilizers, phenothiazines, alcohol), antidepressants, antibiotics (tetracycline, doxycycline, chloramphenicol), the antifungal griseofulvin, sulfa drugs, steroid drugs, oral contraceptives, theophylline, and aminophylline.
- Some of the forms of phenobarbital contain a dye called *tartrazine*, which may cause allergic-type reactions (including bronchial asthma) in some people, especially those sensitive to aspirin.

Other:
- If this drug causes your child to become drowsy, do not allow him or her to engage in activities that require alertness, such as bike riding, swimming, skateboarding, or tree climbing.
- Do not increase or change the prescribed dosage without consulting your doctor.
- Do not stop giving this drug suddenly; if your child has been taking phenobarbital for an extended period of time, the drug must be stopped gradually.
- Never forget that this drug can be habit-forming.

Medical Tests: Your doctor may want to conduct tests to monitor the therapy. This may be especially necessary if your child begins to undergo puberty, which causes the body to use the drug differently. Phenobarbitol may also affect the results of some blood and urine tests, especially those for liver function.

PREDNISONE (GENERIC)

Ingredient(s): prednisone

Equivalent Product(s): Cortan, Deltasone, Fernisone, Liquid Pred, Meticorten, Orasone, Panasol, Prednicen-M, SK-Prednisone, Sterapred

Used For: treatment of inflammation caused by allergies or diseases, including asthma. It is also used to treat disorders of the glandular (endocrine) system.

Dosage Form and Strength: tablets—1 mg, 2.5 mg, 5 mg, 19 mg, 20 mg, 25 mg, 50 mg; syrup—5 mg per 5 ml

Storage: Store away from light in a tightly closed container.

Before Using This Medication Tell Your Doctor: if your child has a history of liver or kidney disease; ulcer or stomach problems; tuberculosis; bone disease; diabetes; seizures; blood or heart disorders; any infection, especially fungal; herpes simplex infection in the eyes; or an underactive thyroid gland. Also tell your doctor about any drugs, prescription or nonprescription, your child is using (especially aspirin; diabetes medicine, including insulin; anticonvulsants; and antibiotics) and about any allergies your child has or any family history of allergies.

This Drug Should Not Be Used If: your child has an allergy to its ingredient, a body-wide infection, or has recently received an immunization or vaccination.

How to Use: Give this drug with food or milk. If your child is taking a single dose each day or each alternate day, give the dose before 9:00 A.M. Multiple daily doses should be given at evenly spaced intervals throughout the day. Do not stop giving this drug without talking to your doctor.

PREDNISONE (GENERIC) (*continued*)

Time Required for Drug to Take Effect: Benefits may be apparent in 24 to 48 hours. The dosage may then have to be adjusted to provide maximum benefit; this usually occurs in four to 10 days. If your child is taking prednisone on a long-term basis, it is important to adjust the dosage so that the smallest possible dose that will still achieve the necessary effect is given.

Missing a Dose: If your are giving the dose once a day, give the missed dose as soon as you remember. If you do not remember until the next day, do not give the missed dose at all, but follow your regular schedule. If your child is taking prednisone every other day, give the missed dose as soon as you remember. If you miss the scheduled time by an entire day, go ahead and give the dose but then skip a day before resuming the regular schedule. Do not double the dose. If your child is taking prednisone more than once a day, give the missed dose as soon as possible and return to the regular schedule. If it is time or almost time for the next dose, double the dose. If you miss more than one dose, call your doctor for instructions.

Symptoms of Overdose: fluid retention, swelling of hands and feet, confusion, anxiety, depression, nervousness, stomach cramping or pain, flushed face, behavior changes, severe headache, convulsions

Side Effects:

Minor and expected:
- nervousness, restlessness, sleeping problems, indigestion, increased susceptibility to bruising and infections, weight gain, increased sweating, dizziness

Serious adverse reactions (CALL YOUR DOCTOR):
- blurred vision, increased thirst, frequent urination, skin rash, unusual bruising, convulsions, mood changes,

PREDNISONE (GENERIC) *(continued)*

slow healing of wounds, sores in the mouth, muscle weakness or pain, bloody or black tarry stools, nausea, vomiting, severe indigestion, unusual fatigue, menstrual irregularities, swelling of legs or feet or face, increased hair growth, unexplained fever or sore throat, irregular heartbeat

Effects of Long-Term Use: slowing of growth and development in children, weight gain, thinning of skin, loss of bone strength resulting in possible fractures, increase in blood sugar (possibly leading to diabetes), eye problems

Habit-Forming Possibility: Long-term use may lead to functional dependence, in which a body function becomes dependent on the drug to do the job of the function. If the drug is withdrawn, that body function is not able to reestablish itself.

Precautions and Suggestions:

Foods and beverages:
- During long-term use a high-protein diet is recommended. Ask your doctor if your child should also eat more potassium-rich foods.

Other Medicines, Prescription or OTC:
- Prednisone interacts with aspirin, phenobarbital, tuberculosis drugs, ephedrine, phenytoin, some antibiotics, and oral contraceptives.
- This drug increases the need for insulin in diabetics.
- There is a possibility that the effects of the bronchodilator theophylline may be increased if prednisone is given at the same time, but the evidence is not conclusive.
- Prednisone is a steroid drug and is powerful. Be certain to tell your doctor about any drugs or products, even something as common as aspirin, that your child is taking when prednisone is prescribed.

PREDNISONE (GENERIC) (*continued*)

Other:
- Do not stop giving this medicine suddenly. If prednisone is to be stopped, it must be stopped gradually, under careful medical supervision. If the use of this drug has caused functional dependency, stopping it abruptly does not give the body time to redevelop its functions.
- Do not give your child more than the prescribed dose, and be certain to follow your doctor's instructions carefully.
- Do not allow your child to receive an immunization or vaccination while taking prednisone.
- If your child is treated by any doctor or dentist, particularly if the treatment involves surgery, within a year of taking prednisone, tell the medical provider that your child was or still is taking prednisone.
- If your child is taking this drug for more than a short-term (one-week) treatment, he or she should wear or carry a medical identification notice that he or she is taking a steroid drug.
- Your child may require higher doses of prednisone during times of stress or illness.
- This drug may mask the signs of infection or allow infections to develop. Watch your child for any sign of illness.

Medical Tests: Your doctor may want to check your child's blood pressure, weight, and vision at regular intervals while prednisone is being given. Your doctor will also watch and test your child's growth and development during treatment. Other laboratory tests may be required to monitor your child's progress. Prednisone can affect the results of some thyroid tests.

PROVENTIL

Ingredient(s): albuterol

Equivalent Product(s): Ventolin

Used For: the relief of spasms in the airways of persons with reversible, obstructive airway conditions, such as asthma or bronchitis

Dosage Form and Strength: tablets—2 mg, 4 mg; inhaler— 90 mcg (micrograms) per actuation

Storage: Store tablets in a dark, cool place. Store inhaler away from heat or open flame. Do not puncture, break, or burn an inhaler.

Before Using This Medication Tell Your Doctor: if your child has any circulatory system problems, a history of seizures, or diabetes. Tell your doctor if your child is using any other bronchodilators, including nonprescription, especially those containing epinephrine. Tell your doctor about any drugs, prescription or nonprescription, your child is taking and about any allergies your child has or any family history of allergies.

This Drug Should Not Be Used If: your child is under 12 years old, has an allergy to the active ingredient in the drug, or has a history of circulatory system problems.

How to Use: If stomach upset occurs, give the treatment along with food.

Time Required for Drug to Take Effect: tablets—within 30 minutes; inhaler—within 15 minutes.

Missing a Dose: If you miss giving a dose by an hour or less, give it when you remember and return to the regular schedule for the next dose. If you miss by more than an hour, wait until the next scheduled dose. Do not double

PROVENTIL (*continued*)

dose, and do not exceed recommended dosage for the entire day.

Symptoms of Overdose: pounding heart, irregular heartbeat, chest pain, fever, chills, cold sweats, paleness, nausea, vomiting, unusual dilation of the pupil of the eye, anxiety, tremors, convulsions, delirium, collapse

Side Effects:

Minor and expected:
- dry throat and mouth, nervousness, stomach upset, unusual taste in mouth

Serious adverse reactions (CALL YOUR DOCTOR):
- pounding heart, chest pain, heartbeat irregularities, dizziness, headache, trembling, flushing, persistent breathing difficulty, confusion, muscle cramps, vomiting, weakness

Effects of Long-Term Use: Tolerance to the drug may develop with prolonged use, but temporarily stopping the drug restores the drug's effectiveness. Discuss this with your doctor.

Habit-Forming Possibility: none known

Precautions and Suggestions:

Foods and beverages:
- no restrictions

Other Medicines, Prescription or OTC:
- This drug may react with other bronchodilators, some antidepressants, some antihistamines, and some heart medicines.

Other:
- Give this drug only as instructed. Do not increase the dosage or give it more often than prescribed without consulting your doctor.

PROVENTIL (*continued*)

- If your child's symptoms do not improve or become worse while using this drug, call your doctor.
- Be certain your child knows how to use the inhaler. Ask your doctor and pharmacist for complete instructions.

Medical Tests: no known interactions

RITALIN

Ingredient(s): methylphenidate

Equivalent Product(s): methylphenidate (generic)

Used For: treatment of attention deficit disorder (hyperactivity)

Dosage Form and Strength: tablets—5 mg, 10 mg, 20 mg; sustained-release tablet—20 mg

Storage: Store at room temperature.

Before Using This Medication Tell Your Doctor: if your child has a psychosis, high blood pressure, or a history of seizures. Tell your doctor about any drugs, prescription or nonprescription, your child is taking and about any allegies your child has or any family history of allergies.

This Drug Should Not Be Used If: your child is allergic to its ingredient or is unusually tense, anxious, or agitated. This drug should not be given to children under the age of six years.

How to Use: Give the medication with food or give the drug with a full glass of water 30 to 45 minutes before a meal. The sustained-release tablet must be swallowed whole.

Time Required for Drug to Take Effect: It may take up to one month before effects are noted.

Missing a Dose: If you remember within an hour of the regular time, give the dose to the child and return to your regular schedule. However, if more than an hour has passed, omit the missed dose and return to the regular dosing schedule. Do not double the next dose.

Symptoms of Overdose: vomiting, agitation, muscle twitches, tremors, convulsions, confusion, delirium, sweating, headache, heartbeat irregularities, dilated pupils, high fever

RITALIN (*continued*)

Side Effects:

Minor and expected:
- loss of appetite, dizziness, drowsiness, headache, nausea, stomach pain, dry mouth

Serious adverse reactions (CALL YOUR DOCTOR):
- insomnia, heartbeat irregularities, nervousness, vomiting, fever, skin rash, convulsions, vision problems, uncontrolled muscle movements, unusual fatigue, unusual mood swings, unexplained sore throat and fever, joint pain

Effects of Long-Term Use: weight loss, possible suppression of growth

Habit-Forming Possibility: Incorrect use of this drug can lead to a tolerance of it and to a mental dependence that may cause abnormal behavior. Withdrawal from the drug should be supervised.

Precautions and Suggestions:

Foods and beverages:
- have your child avoid foods high in tyramine, including ripened, aged cheese; broad bean pods; yeast; and chicken liver. Ask your doctor about other foods.

Other Medicines, Prescription or OTC:
- Ritalin may interact with anticonvulsants (Dilantin, phenobarbital) and with some antidepressants.

Other:
- If this drug causes drowsiness, be sure your child is careful while riding a bicycle or engaging in other activities that require alertness.
- Do not stop giving this drug suddenly and do not increase the dosage without your doctor's approval.

RITALIN (*continued*)

- Your doctor may suggest "drug holidays" for your child during which your child is taken off the drug to see if he or she still needs it and to evaluate his or her growth.
- This drug should not be given indefinitely; it is usually unnecessary after puberty.

Medical Tests: Your doctor may want to perform periodic blood tests while your child is taking Ritalin to assess the effects of the drug. Ritalin may affect the results of some urine tests.

TETRACYCLINE

Ingredient(s): tetracycline hydrochloride

Equivalent Product(s): Achromycin V, Cycine-250, Cyclopar, Deltamycin, Nor-Tet, Panmycin, Retet, Robitet, SK-Tetracycline, Sumycin, Tetra-C, Tetracap, Tetracyn, Tetralan, Tetram

Used For: treatment of bacterial infections and acne

Dosage Form and Strength: oral suspension—125 mg per 5 ml; capsules—100 mg, 250 mg, 500 mg; tablets—250 mg, 500 mg

Storage: Store in a cool, dark place.

Before Using This Medication Tell Your Doctor: if your child has diabetes, liver or kidney disease, or a history of aspirin sensitivity. Tell your doctor about any drugs, prescription or nonprescription, your child is taking and about any allergies your child has or any family history of allergies.

This Drug Should Not Be Used If: your child is allergic to its ingredient. Tetracycline should not be used for children under eight years of age.

How to Use: This drug should be given on an empty stomach at least one hour before or two hours after a meal. Give the dose with a full glass of water. Do not allow the child to take an antacid or any medication containing iron within three hours of a dose. Do not allow your child to eat or drink any dairy products within two hours before or after taking a dose. Continue giving the medication for the full time prescribed by your doctor even if your child seems well.

Time Required for Drug to Take Effect: varies, depending on the infection, but usually two to five days. Acne treatment may be long-term.

TETRACYCLINE (continued)

Missing a Dose: Give the missed dose immediately. If you do not remember until almost time for the next dose, give that dose about halfway through the regular interval between doses. For example, if you are to give a dose at 8:00, 12:00, 4:00, and 8:00, and you remember at 7:00 P.M. that you forgot the 4:00 P.M. dose, give the missed dose at 7:00 P.M. but wait until 9:30 or 10:00 P.M. to give the 8:00 P.M. dose. Then return to the normal schedule. Do not skip a dose or double the dose.

Symptoms of Overdose: possible nausea, vomiting, diarrhea

Side Effects:

Minor and expected:
• sensitivity to sunlight, loss of appetite, diarrhea, upset stomach, nausea, vomiting

Serious adverse reactions (CALL YOUR DOCTOR):
• dark-colored or swollen tongue, rash, hives, itching, difficulty in swallowing, sore throat, sores in mouth, discolored nails, itching in genital and anal areas, fever, joint pain, difficulty in breathing

Effects of Long-Term Use: superinfection—a second infection in addition to the infection being treated. A superinfection is caused by bacteria and other organisms that are not susceptible to or affected by the drug being used to treat the original infection. Thus, these organisms, which are normally too few in number to cause problems, grow unchecked and cause a second infection that may require a different drug to treat.

Habit-Forming Possibility: none

TETRACYCLINE (*continued*)

Precautions and Suggestions:

Foods and beverages:
- Food and dairy products (milk and cheese) interfere with the absorption of tetracycline. Do not give your child dairy products within two hours before or after a dose.

Other Medicines, Prescription or OTC:
- This drug interacts with penicillin, antacids, anticonvulsants, and theophylline (for asthma).
- This drug also interacts with some anesthetics. If your child undergoes any procedure that requires an anesthetic, be sure to tell the doctor or dentist that your child is taking tetracycline.

Other:
- Do not use this drug beyond the expiration date and do not use it if it changes color or appearance. Outdated tetracycline can be poisonous.
- Some forms of this drug contain a dye called *tartrazine* that may cause an allergic reaction, especially in someone who is sensitive to aspirin.
- Don't allow your child to be exposed to sunlight without protective clothing and a sunscreen.
- Tetracycline should not be given to children under the age of eight years nor should it be taken by females who are pregnant or breastfeeding. Tetracycline may cause permanent discoloration of the teeth if it is absorbed during the period of tooth formation—from the last half of the mother's pregnancy through the eighth year of life. It can also affect the development of the teeth and bones in young children.

Medical Tests: In long-term therapy your doctor may want to perform blood tests and liver and kidney tests. Tetracycline can affect the results of some urine tests.

THEOPHYLLINE (GENERIC)

Ingredient(s): theophylline

Equivalent Product(s): Accurbron, Aerolate, Aquaphyllin, Asmalix, Bronkodyl, Constant-T, Duraphyl, Elixicon, Elixomin, Elixophyllin, LaBID, Lanophyllin, Liquophylline, Lixolin, Lodrane, Quibron-T Dividose, Respbid, Slobid, Slo-Phyllin, Somophyllin-T, Sustaire, Theo-24, Theobid, Theobron, Theoclear, Theo-Dur, Theolair, Theo-Lix, Theolixir, Theon, Theophyl, Theospan, Theostat, Theo-Time, Theovent, Uniphyl

Used For: treatment of breathing problems in asthma or chronic bronchitis

Dosage Form and Strength: capsules—50 mg, 100 mg, 200 mg, 250 mg; chewable tablets—100 mg; tablets—100 mg, 125 mg, 200 mg, 225 mg, 250 mg, 300 mg; elixir—80 mg, 112.5 mg, both per 15 ml; solution—80 mg per 15 ml; liquid—80 mg, 150 mg, 160 mg, all per 15 ml; syrup—80 mg, 150 mg, both per 15 ml; suspension—300 mg per 15 ml; timed-release capsules—50 mg, 60 mg, 65 mg, 75 mg, 100 mg, 125 mg, 130 mg, 200 mg, 250 mg, 260 mg, 300 mg, 400 mg, 500 mg

Storage: Store in a dry, tightly covered container.

Before Using This Medication Tell Your Doctor: if your child has any form of heart, liver, or kidney disease; inflammation of the stomach or an ulcer; or sensitivity to caffeine. Also, tell your doctor about any drugs, prescription or nonprescription, your child is taking and about any allergies your child has or any family history of allergies.

This Drug Should Not Be Used If: your child is allergic to this drug or any similar drugs, has an ulcer or other stomach inflammation, or is sensitive to caffeine.

THEOPHYLLINE (GENERIC)

(*continued*)

How to Use: Theophylline is more effective if taken on an empty stomach; however, if stomach upset occurs, give it with food. If possible, give with a full glass of water one hour before or two hours after a meal. Give every six hours around the clock, except for timed-release capsules. Do not crush, or allow child to chew, coated or timed-released forms.

Time Required for Drug to Take Effect: The effect begins within 15 to 30 minutes and reaches a maximum benefit in one to two hours. Depending on the dosage form and strength, the drug's benefit begins to subside in six to ten hours.

Missing a Dose: If you remember the missed dose within an hour of its normally scheduled time, give the missed dose. Then return to your normal schedule. If more than an hour has passed since the normally scheduled time, wait until the next regular dose. Do not double the dose. Ask your doctor about what to do for your individual situation if you miss a dose.

Symptoms of Overdose: loss of appetite, nausea, restlessness, irritability, occasional vomiting, headache, confusion. Children especially may display restlessness and hyperactivity that may precede convulsions. *Sometimes with children a large overdose may lead to convulsions and death without warning symptoms of poisoning.*

Side Effects:

Minor and expected:
• nervousness, insomnia

Serious adverse reactions (CALL YOUR DOCTOR):
• vomiting, skin rashes or hives, irregular heartbeat, stomach pain, rapid breathing, severe depression, ab-

THEOPHYLLINE (GENERIC)

(*continued*)

normal behavior (withdrawal alternating with hyperactivity), headache, confusion, restlessness, nausea, loss of appetite, irritability, convulsions, breathing difficulty, loss of body fluids, thirst, fever

Effects of Long-Term Use: stomach irritation

Habit-Forming Possibility: none

Precautions and Suggestions:

Foods and beverages:
- Have your child avoid charcoal-broiled food and a high-protein/low-carbohydrate diet. Try to balance your child's diet between high-protein/low-carbohydrate and low-protein/high-carbohydrate, either of which can affect the way the body uses and eliminates theophylline. Also, do not permit your child to eat or drink large amounts of anything containing caffeine or chocolate (don't forget that many colas contain caffeine). Ask your doctor for suggestions about the most beneficial diet for your child.

Other Medicines, Prescription or OTC:
- Theophylline interacts with other drugs for asthma, including ephedrine (used in some nasal decongestants); phenobarbital; some antibiotics (erythromycin, troleandomycin, clindamycin); the ulcer medication cimetidine; some antacids; and the anticonvulsant Dilantin.
- Theophylline may interact with the worm medicine called thiabendazole.
- If your doctor recommends a flu vaccination for your child, remind the doctor that the child is taking theophylline, which can interact with a flu vaccination.
- Theophylline can interact with some anesthetics; if your child faces any procedure that requires anesthe-

THEOPHYLLINE (GENERIC)

(continued)

sia, be sure to tell the doctor or dentist that the child is taking theophylline.
- Always consult your doctor before giving your child any other medicines, including over-the-counter products.

Other:
- If theophylline is prescribed for your teen-ager who smokes tobacco or marijuana, tell your doctor of your child's smoking habits. Smoking can affect the action of this drug.

Medical Tests: This drug may affect the results of some urine tests. Usage is monitored by measuring blood levels; short-acting theophylline is monitored two hours after the dose is given, and the long-acting form is measured four hours after the dose is given.

TOFRANIL

Ingredient(s): imipramine hydrochloride

Equivalent Product(s): imipramine hydrochloride (generic), Janimine, SK-Pramine, Tipramine

Used For: control of bed-wetting in children six years of age or older

Dosage Form and Strength: tablets—10 mg, 25 mg, 50 mg

Storage: Store in a tightly closed container at room temperature.

Before Using This Medication Tell Your Doctor: if your child has a history of heart, kidney, or liver disease or of seizures or diabetes. Also inform your doctor if your child is sensitive to aspirin. Tell your doctor about any drugs, prescription or nonprescription, your child is taking and about any allergies your child has or any family history of allergies.

This Drug Should Not Be Used If: your child is allergic to its ingredient or is under six years of age.

How to Use: Give your child the medicine with water or food to lessen the chance of upset stomach. Tofranil should be given about an hour before bedtime, or, in the case of early evening bed-wetters, in a smaller dose starting at midday.

Time Required for Drug to Take Effect: varies, depending on the child and the severity of the problem.

Missing a Dose: If you miss a once-a-day bedtime dose, do not give that dose in the morning. Call your doctor for instructions. Never double the dose, and do not stop giving the drug without the advice of a physician; abrupt discontinuation may cause nausea, headache, and a run-down feeling.

TOFRANIL (continued)

Symptoms of Overdose: Children are more sensitive to overdose of this drug than are adults. Observe your child
carefully while he or she is using this medication. Symptoms include confusion, agitation, hallucinations, seizures, high fever, flushing, dry mouth, dilated pupils,
and irregular heartbeat. (There is a capsule form of this
drug called Tofranil-PM that is more potent than the
tablets and therefore should not be used by children
because of the increased risk of overdose.)

Side Effects:

Minor and expected:
•nervousness, sleep disorders, tiredness, lethargy, mild
upset stomach, sensitivity to sunlight.

Serious adverse reactions (CALL YOUR DOCTOR):
• convulsions, anxiety, emotional reactions, dry mouth,
fainting, collapse

Effects of Long-Term Use: none reported

Habit-Forming Possibility: rare

Precautions and Suggestions:

Foods and beverages:
• no restrictions

Other Medicines, Prescription or OTC:
• This drug may increase the effects of tranquilizers,
antihistamines, and narcotic medications.
• Do not give your child any medications, over-the-
counter or prescription, for colds, coughs, or sinus
problems.
• This drug interacts with methylphenidate (Ritalin), often
prescribed for children with attention deficit disorder
(hyperactivity).

TOFRANIL (*continued*)

- Tofranil contains a dye called *tartrazine* that may cause allergic-type reactions (including bronchial asthma) in some people, especially those sensitive to aspirin.

Other:
- If this drug causes your child to be drowsy, do not permit him or her to climb trees, ride a bicycle, or engage in other activities that require alertness.
- Do not allow your child to be exposed to sunlight or sunlamps for prolonged periods of time because of the possibility of increased sensitivity to sunlight.
- This drug should be discontinued before any surgery or before some X rays using certain radiopaque dye. Tell your doctor or dentist recommending these procedures that your child is taking this medication.
- Tofranil's effects may continue up to seven days after your child has stopped taking it, so continue to observe all precautions.

Medical Tests: Tofranil interferes with laboratory urine tests. Your doctor may want to perform periodic blood tests to monitor your child's progress while taking this drug.

TRI-VI-FLOR

Ingredient(s): vitamin A, vitamin D, vitamin C, fluoride

Equivalent Product(s): Tri-Bay-Flor, Tri-Vitamin with Fluoride, Vi-Daylin

Used For: a vitamin and fluoride supplement

Dosage Form and Strength: chewable tablets—2,500 IU vitamin A, 400 IU vitamin D, 60 mg vitamin C, 1 mg flouride; drops—1,500 IU vitamin A, 400 IU vitamin D, 35 mg vitamin C, 0.5 mg fluoride

Storage: Store at room temperature only in its original plastic container.

Before Using This Medication Tell Your Doctor: if your child has any allergies or illnesses. Also tell your doctor about any other drugs, prescription or nonprescription, that you are giving your child.

This Drug Should Not Be Used If: your child is allergic to it and if the drinking water where you live is flouridated 0.3 ppm or more. Call your local health department to find out about your local drinking water.

How to Use: You can administer the prescribed liquid dosage by gently releasing the drops into the child's cheek, or you can mix it with a little food or fluid. To prevent an upset stomach, give the medication with food, but not at the same time as dairy foods. Milk and other dairy products may decrease absorption of the medication.

Time Required for Drug to Take Effect: not applicable

Missing a Dose: Give the missed dose as soon as you remember unless it is almost time for the next dose. In that case, don't give the missed dose, but return to your regular dosing schedule.

TRI-VI-FLOR *(continued)*

Symptoms of Overdose: severe stomach uspet, excessive salivation, mottled discoloration of teeth.

Side Effects:

Minor and expected:
• none if given in the proper dosages

Serious adverse reactions (CALL YOUR DOCTOR):
• severe stomach upset, excessive salivation, mottling of teeth, black stools, diarrhea, bloody vomit, nausea, drowsiness, fainting, unusual excitement, constipation, aching bones, rash, sores in mouth, stiffness, weight loss, loss of appetite

Effects of Long-Term Use: prevention of tooth decay

Habit-Forming Possibility: none

Precautions and Suggestions:

Foods and beverages:
• Do not give this medication at the same time as your child is consuming dairy products.

Other Medicines, Prescription or OTC:
• no interactions

Other:
• If you move to a different area, discontinue use until you determine whether or not the drinking water in your new home is flouridated.

Medical Tests: no interactions

VERMOX

Ingredient(s): mebendazole

Equivalent Product(s): none

Used For: treatment of whipworm, pinworm, roundworm, common hookworm, or American hookworm

Dosage Form and Strength: chewable tablets—100 mg

Storage: Store in a tightly closed container at room temperature.

Before Using This Medication Tell Your Doctor: if your child is taking any other drugs, prescription or nonprescription, or has any allergies or any family history of allergies.

This Drug Should Not Be Used If: your child is allergic to its ingredient.

How to Use: This drug may be chewed, swallowed, or crushed and mixed with food. If the medication is mixed with food, the child must eat all of the food to receive the full dose of medication. This drug's safety and effectiveness in treating children under the age of two years has not been established. You and your doctor must consider the benefits of the drug versus any possible risk for such children.

Time Required for Drug to Take Effect: Your child should be cured within three weeks after the beginning of the treatment.

Missing a Dose: Ask your doctor for instructions. For some worms, only a single tablet is given once. To treat other types of infestations you may have to give your child one tablet in the morning and one in the evening on three consecutive days. Your doctor can advise you about the dosage schedule.

Symptoms of Overdose: fever

VERMOX (*continued*)

Side Effects:

Minor and expected:
- brief and passing abdominal pain and diarrhea in cases of massive infestation and excretion of worms.

Serious adverse reactions (CALL YOUR DOCTOR):
- fever

Effects of Long-Term Use: not applicable

Habit-Forming Possibility: none

Precautions and Suggestions:

Foods and beverages:
- no restrictions

Other Medicines, Prescription or OTC:
- no restrictions

Other:
- Because worm infestations, especially pinworm invasions, are easily passed from one family member to another, your doctor will probably recommend that all members of your household be treated to eliminate the worms completely. Extremely careful hygiene is critically important to the prevention of reinfestation; change and wash underwear, nightclothes, bed linens, and towels every day. Disinfect toilets and bathrooms daily as well.

Medical Tests: no known interferences

12

OVER-THE-COUNTER DRUGS

AFRIN

Ingredient(s): oxymetazoline hydrochloride

Equivalent Product(s): Bayfrin, Dristan Long Lasting, Duramist Plus, Duration, 4-Way Long Acting Nasal, Neo-Synephrine 12 Hour, Nostrilla, NTZ Long Acting Nasal Drops, oxymetazoline (generic), Sinex Long-Lasting

Used For: temporary relief of stuffy nose

Dosage Form and Strength: solution—0.025% (for children from two to six years of age), 0.05%

Storage: Store at room temperature

This Drug Should Not Be Used If: your child is allergic to its ingredient or has a history of diabetes, ulcers, or heart disease. This product is not recommended for children under two years of age.

How to Use: Drop two or three drops into each nostril in the morning and the evening. Do not use for more than three days in a row; using this product any longer may worsen the stuffiness.

Missing a Dose: Give the missed dose and then wait for about 12 hours to give the next dose. Maintain the new schedule.

Side Effects:

Minor and expected:
- stinging, burning, sneezing, dry nose, headache, rapid heartbeat

Serious adverse reactions (CALL YOUR DOCTOR):
- chronic swelling of membranes of the nose after prolonged or excessive use; also sweating, drowsiness, deep sleep or sleeplessness, nervousness, dizziness, heartbeat irregularities

AFRIN (continued)

Effects of Long-Term Use: see "Serious adverse reactions,"
   above

Habit-Forming Possibility: none

Precautions and Suggestions:
   • Do not use this solution in sprayers or containers with
     parts made of aluminum, which reacts with the drug.
   • Discoloration of the product means that it has decom-
     posed. Discard it.
   • Don't allow more than one person to use the same
     container.
   • Rinse dropper or spray tip in hot water after each use.

BENYLIN

Ingredient(s): diphenhydramine hydrochloride

Equivalent Product(s): Benadryl

Used For: control of cough, allergy-related itching and swelling of skin, motion sickness

Dosage Form and Strength: syrup—12.5 mg per 5 ml

Storage: Store at room temperature.

This Drug Should Not Be Used If: your child is allergic to its ingredient, has a history of heart disease or ulcers, or has asthma or another lower respiratory tract condition. This drug should not be used to treat any lung condition. This drug should not be given to infants.

How to Use: Give the child one medical teaspoon every four hours, not to exceed 50 mg in 24 hours. Give the dose with water, food, or milk to reduce stomach upset.

Missing a Dose: Give the missed dose as soon as possible. If it is almost time for the next dose, however, omit the missed dose and return to the regular schedule.

Side Effects:

Minor and expected:
- dry mouth, nose, or throat, dizziness, drowsiness, sensitivity to sunlight, nasal congestion, thickening of lung secretions, wheezing, headache, frequent urination, upset stomach, vomiting, diarrhea, constipation

Serious adverse reactions (CALL YOUR DOCTOR):
- excited state (especially in young children), rash, chills, painful or difficult urination, blurred vision, pounding heartbeat, confusion, clumsiness, unexplained sore throat, severe headache, fever, tightness in chest, tingling and weakness in the hands, convulsions

BENYLIN (*continued*)

Effects of Long-Term Use: This drug should not be used for a long period of time. Benylin is used to treat short-term symptoms. Long-term use can lead to a form of anemia, a deficiency of red blood cells.

Habit-Forming Possibility: none

Precautions and Suggestions:

- A persistent cough may be a sign of a serious illness. If your child's cough lasts longer than one week, stop giving this medication and call your doctor.
- Give this and any cough preparation only if it is really needed, such as when your child cannot sleep because of constant coughing. A cough is a defense mechanism and should be allowed to occur if it does not cause undue discomfort.
- If your child becomes drowsy, do not allow him or her to engage in activities that require alertness, such as bike riding, swimming, tree climbing, or skateboard riding.
- Do not give Benylin at the same time as you are giving your child a tranquilizer or sedative.

CALAMINE LOTION (GENERIC)

Ingredient(s): zinc oxide, calamine, glycerin

Equivalent Product(s): various and numerous generic equivalents

Used For: temporary relief of itching and pain of minor skin irritations

Dosage Form and Strength: lotion—8% zinc oxide, 8% calamine, 0.2% glycerin

Storage: Store at room temperature.

This Drug Should Not Be Used If: your child is allergic to its ingredients. Do not apply it to large, raw, oozing areas.

How to Use: Shake the bottle well. (It may be necessary to shake it again from time to time as you use the lotion because the mixture settles rather quickly.) Apply the lotion two to four times daily and at bedtime. If you are using it on a blistery rash (for example, chicken pox), dab it on gently with a cotton ball to avoid breaking open the rash spots.

Missing a Dose: not applicable

Side Effects: none known

Effects of Long-Term Use: Your child may become sensitive to the ingredients in the lotion.

Habit-Forming Possibility: none

Precautions and Suggestions:

- Do not use calamine lotion containing phenol for babies or when treating rashes accompanied by open

CALAMINE LOTION
(GENERIC) (*continued*)

sores. Phenol can be irritating, and it rates low in effectiveness.
- Do not use in or around the eyes, or other mucous membranes, on the genital area, or on infected areas.
- Do not use calamine lotion for an extended period of time.

CLEARASIL

Ingredient(s): benzoyl peroxide

Equivalent Product(s): Benoxyl-5, benzoyl peroxide (generic), Dry and Clear, Oxy-5, Persadox, Zeroxin

Used For: treatment of mild to moderate acne

Dosage Form and Strength: lotion—5%

Storage: Store at room temperature.

This Drug Should Not Be Used If: your child is allergic to its ingredient.

How to Use: After washing the skin, smooth a small amount of Clearasil over the affected area. Apply once daily for the first few days. If side effects do not occur in three or four days, increase the applications to twice daily. If unusual stinging or burning occurs after an application, wash away the Clearasil with mild soap and water and then apply again the next day.

Missing a Dose: not applicable

Side Effects:

> *Minor and expected:*
> * slight stinging and/or warmth upon application, dryness, peeling
>
> *Serious adverse reactions (CALL YOUR DOCTOR):*
> * excessive scaling, redness, or swelling of the skin

Effects of Long-Term Use: No ill effects should be noticed if there is no allergy to the product.

Habit-Forming Possibility: none

Precautions and Suggestions:

> * Keep this medication away from the eyes, creases around the sides of nose, mouth, and other mucous membranes. Also keep away from hair.

CLEARASIL (*continued*)

- This product may damage certain fabrics, especially colored fabrics and rayon.
- Your child can use regular cosmetics without risk of interaction with Clearasil.
- While using Clearasil, avoid the use of harsh, abrasive cleansers on the affected skin.
- Do not allow your child to be exposed to heat lamps, sunlamps, or sunlight for prolonged periods while using this medication.

DESITIN

Ingredient(s): zinc oxide, cod liver oil, and talc in a petrolatum/lanolin base

Equivalent Product(s): none

Used For: prevention and treatment of diaper rash and other minor skin irritations.

Dosage Form and Strength: available in tubes of one, two, four, eight, and 16 ounces

Storage: Store at room temperature.

This Drug Should Not Be Used If: your child is allergic to any of its ingredients.

How to Use: Apply Desitin to the affected area three or four times daily as needed. You can prevent diaper rash by applying this product at each diaper change. It is especially helpful to apply it to the diaper area at bedtime, when the baby will be wearing the same diaper for a long period of time.

Missing a Dose: not applicable

Side Effects: none

Effects of Long-Term Use: prevents diaper rash

Habit-Forming Possibility: none

Precautions and Suggestions: none

DIMETANE

Ingredient(s): phenylephrine hydrochloride, brompheniramine maleate

Equivalent Product(s): none

Used For: relief of symptoms accompanying upper respiratory conditions, such as runny or stuffy nose, congestion, watering eyes

Dosage Form and Strength: elixir—5 mg phenylephrine hydrochloride, 2 mg brompheniramine maleate, 2.3% alcohol

Storage: Store at room temperature.

This Drug Should Not Be Used If: your child is allergic to its ingredients or has a history of high blood pressure, asthma, heart disease, or diabetes. This drug is not recommended for children under two years of age.

How to Use: Give your two- to five-year-old child ½ teaspoon every four hours, not to exceed three teaspoons in 24 hours. Children ages six to 12 years should receive one teaspoon every four hours, not to exceed six teaspoons in 24 hours. Children over 12 years old can take two teaspoons every four hours, not to exceed 12 teaspoons in 24 hours.

Missing a Dose: Give the missed dose when you remember and then wait four hours to give the next dose. Maintain this new schedule.

Side Effects:

> *Minor and expected:*
> • drowsiness
>
> *Serious adverse reactions (CALL YOUR DOCTOR):*
> • nervousness, dizziness, sleeplessness, excitability

DIMETANE (*continued*)

Effects of Long-Term Use: Using this drug for more than three to five days may cause the symptoms it is intended to relieve to worsen instead.

Habit-Forming Possibility: none

Precautions and Suggestions:

- If this drug causes your child to become drowsy, do not allow him or her to engage in any activities that require alertness, such as skateboarding, bike riding, swimming, or tree climbing.
- Give this drug for the first time early in the day, so if the child becomes excited or overactive it will not be at bedtime.

DRAMAMINE

Ingredient(s): dimenhydrinate

Equivalent Product(s): Calm X, dimenhydrinate (generic), Dimentabs, Dramaban, Marmine, Motion-Aid

Used For: prevention and treatment of nausea and vomiting of motion sickness

Dosage Form and Strength: tablet—50 mg; liquid—12.5 mg per 4 ml

Storage: Store at room temperature.

This Drug Should Not Be Used If: your child is allergic to its ingredient or has a history of asthma, ulcers, or heart disease. This drug is not recommended for use with a child under two years of age unless monitored by a doctor.

How to Use: Give your two- to six-year-old child up to 25 mg every six to eight hours, not to exceed 75 mg in 24 hours. Give your six- to 12-year-old 25 to 50 mg every six to eight hours, not to exceed 150 mg in 24 hours. For children over 12 years, give 50 to 100 mg every four to six hours, not to exceed 400 mg in 24 hours.

Missing a Dose: Give the missed dose when you remember unless it is almost time for the next dose. Then simply continue on the regular schedule and skip the missed dose. Be certain not to exceed the daily limits for your child's age.

Side Effects:

Minor and expected:
• drowsiness

Serious adverse reactions (CALL YOUR DOCTOR):
• nervousness, confusion, headache, sleeplessness, heaviness and weakness of hands, nausea, vomiting, diar-

DRAMAMINE (*continued*)

rhea, constipation, upset stomach, blurred vision, rash, heartbeat irregularities, stuffy nose, wheezing, tightness in chest, dry mouth and throat

Effects of Long-Term Use: not applicable

Habit-Forming Possibility: none

Precautions and Suggestions:

- This drug can react with certain antibiotics. Talk to your doctor if your child is taking an antibiotic and you want to give this medication.
- If your child becomes drowsy, do not allow him or her to engage in any activities that require alertness. A teen-ager taking this drug should not drive a car or ride a bicycle.

HYDROCORTISONE (GENERIC)

Ingredient(s): hydrocortisone acetate

Equivalent Product(s): Caladryl, CaldeCort, Clinicort, Cortaid, Epifoam, Gynecort, Lanacort, Pharma-Cort, Resicort, Rhulicort

Used For: temporary relief of minor skin irritations—including itching, rashes, insect bites, poison ivy, sumac, and oak—and discomfort caused by soaps, detergents, cosmetics, jewelry, and clothing.

Dosage Form and Strength: ointment—0.5%; cream—0.5%; lotion—0.5%; foam—aerosol, 1%

Storage: Store away from light in a tightly closed container.

This Drug Should Not Be Used If: your child is allergic to its ingredients or to any steroid drugs or has a fungal infection, any other infection, tuberculosis of the skin, chicken pox, shingles, herpes simplex, or a perforated eardrum. It should not be used for children under two years of age.

How to Use: Wash your hands and then wash the affected area with water. Pat dry. Apply the medication in a thin film and rub it in lightly. Do not apply a thick layer. Do not wrap or bandage the area. If you are using the aerosol applicator, do not breathe the vapors or puncture the can. *Do not allow the medication to get into your child's eyes.*

Missing a Dose: Apply the missed dose as soon as you remember. If it is almost time for the next dose, however, do not apply the missed dose but return to the original dosing schedule. Do not apply twice as much medication at the next dose.

HYDROCORTISONE (GENERIC) (*continued*)

Side Effects:

Minor and expected:
- A stinging, burning sensation may occur when this drug is applied; this is harmless.

Serious adverse reactions (CALL YOUR DOCTOR):
- severe burning or stinging; itching, blistering, peeling, or any signs of irritation that were not present when you started to use this drug; increased hair growth; thinning of the skin; loss of skin color; signs of infection on the skin; discoloration of the skin; abnormal lines on the skin

Effects of Long-Term Use: slowing of growth and development in children, weight gain, thinning of skin, easy bruising, loss of bone strength

Habit-Forming Possibility: There probably is none, but long-term use of a steroid drug may lead to functional dependence, in which the body depends on the drug to perform a body function.

Precautions and Suggestions:

- If you are using this medicine in your child's diaper area, do not use a tight-fitting diaper or plastic pants.
- This is a steroid drug and should be used carefully.
- Although this is a low-strength form, in order to be a nonprescription drug, young children can absorb a great deal of the medication through the skin. If the affected area does not seem to be improving, or in fact is becoming worse, discontinue use of the product and consult your doctor.

NEOSPORIN

Ingredient(s): polymyxin B, bacitracin zinc, neomycin sulfate

Equivalent Product(s): none

Used For: first aid to treat or prevent surface bacterial infections of minor cuts, scrapes, or abrasions of the skin.

Dosage Form and Strength: ointment—5,000 units polymyxin, 400 units bacitracin, 5 mg neomycin per gram

Storage: Cap the tube tightly and store at room temperature.

This Drug Should Not Be Used If: your child has an allergy to any of its ingredients or to any other topical antibiotic.

How to Use: Gently wash the affected area and apply the ointment in a thin layer two to five times a day at relatively evenly spaced intervals. Cover the area with sterile gauze if desired. Remove any crusting of the sore area before applying the ointment.

Missing a Dose: Apply the missed dose as soon as you remember and repeat applications at evenly spaced intervals.

Symptoms of Overdose: none known

Side Effects:

   Minor and expected:
   • minor irritation of skin

   Serious adverse reactions (CALL YOUR DOCTOR):
   • swelling, scaling, itching, redness of the skin, persisting or increasing pain at the site, failure of the infection or wound to heal. Neomycin absorbed through large areas of damaged skin may lead to kidney problems or hearing difficulties.

Effects of Long-Term Use: none known; not intended for long-term use

NEOSPORIN (continued)

Habit-Forming Possibility: none

Precautions and Suggestions:

- This drug is not intended to be used for deep puncture wounds, serious burns, deep infections of the skin, or severe cases of impetigo. If any of these conditions applies to your child, see your doctor for more appropriate treatment and/or medicine.
- Neosporin ointment must not be used in the eyes.
- If you have any doubts about how your child is reacting to this medication, call your doctor.

NEO-SYNEPHRINE

Ingredient(s): phenylephrine

Equivalent Product(s): Alconefrin, Allerest, Coricidin Nasal Mist, doktors Nose Drops, Duration Mild, Newphrine, Nostril, Pyracort-D, Rhinall, Sinarest Nasal, Sinex, Sinophen Intranasal, Super Anahist

Used For: temporary relief of stuffy nose

Dosage Form and Strength: solution—0.125%, 0.25%, 0.5% and 1%

Storage: Store at room temperature.

This Drug Should Not Be Used If: your child is allergic to its ingredient or has a history of heart disease or diabetes

How to Use: Place the recommended number of drops in each nostril every three to four hours. The 0.125% solution should be used for children up to six years old. Children over six years should be given the 0.25% solution. Do not use for more than three days in a row; using this product longer may worsen stuffiness.

Missing a Dose: Give the missed dose and then wait three or four hours to give the next dose. Maintain the new schedule.

Side Effects:

Minor and expected:
• stinging, burning, sneezing, dry nose, headache

Serious adverse reactions (CALL YOUR DOCTOR):
• chronic swelling of the membranes of the nose after prolonged or excessive use; also sweating, drowsiness, deep sleep or sleeplessness, nervousness, dizziness, heartbeat irregularities

NEO-SYNEPHRINE (*continued*)

Effects of Long-Term Use: See "Serious adverse reactions," above.

Habit-Forming Possibility: none

Precautions and Suggestions:

- Discoloration of this product means it has decomposed. Discard.
- Don't allow more than one person to use the same container of Neo-Synephrine.
- Rinse the dropper or spray tip in hot water after each use.

NEO-SYNEPHRINE II

Ingredient(s): xylometazoline hydrochloride

Equivalent Product(s): Chlorohist-LA, Corimist, Otrivin, Sinutab Long-Lasting, xylometazoline hydrochloride (generic)

Used For: temporary relief of stuffy nose

Dosage Form and Strength: solution—0.05% (for children under 12 years), 0.1%

Storage: Store at room temperature.

This Drug Should Not Be Used If: your child is allergic to its ingredient or has a history of diabetes, ulcers, or heart disease. This product is not recommended for children under two years of age.

How to Use: Place two or three drops of the 0.05% solution in each nostril every eight to ten hours. Do not use for more than three days in a row; using this product longer may worsen the stuffiness.

Missing a Dose: Give the missed dose and then wait eight to ten hours to give the next dose. Maintain the new schedule.

Side Effects:

   Minor and expected:
   • stinging, burning, sneezing, dry nose, headache, rapid heartbeat

   Serious adverse reactions (CALL YOUR DOCTOR):
   • chronic swelling of membranes of the nose after prolonged or excessive use; also sweating, drowsiness, deep sleep or sleeplessness, nervousness, dizziness, heartbeat irregularities

NEO-SYNEPHRINE II (*continued*)

Effects of Long-Term Use: See "Serious adverse reactions," above.

Habit-Forming Possibility: none

Precautions and Suggestions:

- Do not use this solution in sprayers or containers with any parts made of aluminum, which reacts with the drug.
- Discoloration of the product means it has decomposed and should be discarded.
- Don't allow more than one person to use the same container of medication.
- Rinse the dropper or spray tip in hot water after each use.

NOVAHISTINE

Ingredient(s): phenylephrine, chlorpheniramine

Equivalent Products(s): Bayhistine Elixir, Comhist Liquid, Ru-Tuss Plain Liquid

Used For: relief of symptoms of colds and other upper respiratory conditions

Dosage Form and Strength: elixir—5 mg phenylephrine, 2 mg chlorpheniramine per 5 ml

Storage: Store at room temperature.

This Drug Should Not Be Used If: your child is allergic to its ingredients or has a history of high blood pressure, heart disease, ulcers, asthma, or diabetes. This drug is not recommended for use by children under two years of age.

How to Use: Give children two to five years ½ teaspoon every four hours. For children six to 12 years old, give one teaspoon every four hours. For children over 12 years, give two teaspoons every four hours.

Missing a Dose: Give the missed dose when you remember it and then wait four hours to give the next dose. Maintain the new schedule.

Side Effects:

> *Minor and expected:*
> • drowsiness, dry mouth
>
> *Serious adverse reactions (CALL YOUR DOCTOR):*
> • excitability, nervousness, dizziness, weakness, nausea, vomiting, headache, stomach upset, diccifult or painful urination, restlessness, sleeplessness

Effects of Long-Term Use: Using this drug for more than three to five days may cause the symptoms it is intended to relieve to worsen instead.

NOVAHISTINE (*continued*)

Habit-Forming Possibility: none

Precautions and Suggestions:

- If this drug causes your child to become drowsy, do not allow him or her to engage in activities that require alertness, such as skateboarding, bike riding, tree climbing, or swimming.
- Give this drug for the first time early in the day, so if the child becomes excited or overactive it will not be at bedtime.

NUPRIN

Ingredient(s): ibuprofen

Equivalent Product(s): Advil, (Ibuprofen is also available in higher strengths as the prescription drugs Motrin and Rufen.)

Used For: relief of mild pain associated with arthritis, headache, toothache, muscle aches, backache, menstruation, and the common cold as well as for the reduction of fever.

Dosage Form and Strength: tablet—200 mg

Storage: Store at room temperature and avoid unusually high heat (over 104°).

This Drug Should Not Be Used If: your child is under 12 years of age, is allergic or sensitive to aspirin, or has ever had an allergic reaction to ibuprofen. Do not use this drug for your child if he or she has nasal polyps; a history of ulcers or other stomach problems; kidney, liver or heart disease; high blood pressure; bleeding or clotting problems. If your child is taking any other medicines, prescription or nonprescription, ask your doctor if it is all right to give Nuprin at the same time. Also, if your child is under a doctor's care for a serious condition, check with your doctor before giving this medicine.

How to Use: Give Nuprin on an empty stomach one-half to one hour before or two hours after eating. However, if upset stomach occurs, give the drug with food or milk. Although the drug works faster when taken on an empty stomach, in the long run it is just as effective if taken with food or milk.

Missing a Dose: Give the missed dose as soon as you remember and then continue with the usual schedule. However,

NUPRIN (*continued*)

if it is nearly time for the next dose, skip the missed dose and return to the usual schedule. Do not double the dose.

Side Effects:

Minor and expected:
- Indigestion, nausea, cramping, excessive gas, bloating, diarrhea, constipation, headache, nervousness, loss of appetite

Serious adverse reactions (CALL YOUR DOCTOR):
- Blurred, diminished, and/or changed vision, skin rash, hives, itching, fluid retention resulting in weight gain, bloody or black tarry stools, ringing in the ears, yellowish skin or eyes, decreased hearing, pounding heartbeat, confusion, chills, difficult breathing, unexplained sore throat, fever

Effects of Long-Term Use: possible harmful effect on kidney or liver function

Habit-Forming Possibility: none known

Precautions and Suggestions:

- Do not give this drug if your child is taking another medication that contains alcohol since the combination of ibuprofen and alcohol can increase irritation in the stomach and thus increase the possibility of stomach irritation and bleeding.
- Do not give your child aspirin at the same time as he or she is taking Nuprin.
- This drug may interact with phenobarbital, phenytoin (Dilantin), sulfa drugs, pain medications, and some other medicines.
- If this drug causes nausea or changes in vision, do not allow your child to participate in any activity that

NUPRIN (*continued*)

requires alertness, such as skateboarding, bike riding, swimming, or tree climbing.
- Nuprin's ability to reduce both inflammation and fever can conceal signs of infection. If your child develops any symptoms that may indicate a new or unrelated condition or illness, call your doctor.

PEDIALYTE

Ingredient(s): water, dextrose, potassium citrate, sodium chloride, sodium citrate, citric acid, magnesium chloride, calcium chloride

Equivalent Product(s): none

Used For: replacing water and minerals lost in diarrhea and vomiting

Dosage Form and Strength: liquid with various amounts of minerals available in sizes from 8 ounces to 32 ounces

Storage: Store at room temperature.

This Drug Should Not Be Used If: diarrhea or vomiting is severe. This product should be used for only one or two days.

How to Use: Give the child as much as he or she will take. However, do not give more than four ounces per 2.2 pounds of the child's body weight. Children between five and 10 years of age may require one to two quarts a day. Children older than 10 years may need two to three quarts. It is wise to discuss the use and amount of this product with your doctor.

Missing a Dose: not applicable

Side Effects: none

Effects of Long-Term Use: not applicable

Habit-Forming Possibility: none

Precautions and Suggestions:

- Do not give or mix with other fluids containing minerals, such as milk or fruit juices.

ROBITUSSIN

Ingredient(s): guaifenesin

Equivalent Product(s): Anti-Tuss, Baytussin, Colrex, Cremacoat 2 Liquid, GG-CEN, Glyate, Glycotuss, guaifenesin (generic), Guiamid, Guiatuss, Halotussin, Malotuss, Nortussin, Peedee Dose, Robafen, S-T Expectorant SF & DF

Used For: relief of dry, nonproductive cough

Dosage Form and Strength: syrup—100 mg per 5 ml

Storage: Store this drug at room temperature.

This Drug Should Not Be Used If: your child is allergic to its ingredient. This product should not be used for a chronic cough (such as that caused by asthma) or for a cough that produces a great amount of secretions. You should not give this medication if your child has a high fever, persistent headache, rash, nausea, or vomiting. If those symptoms are present, call your doctor.

How to Use: For children two to five years old, give ½ teaspoon every four hours, not to exceed three teaspoons in 24 hours. For children aged six to 12 years, give ½ teaspoon every four hours, not to exceed six teaspoons in 24 hours. For children over 12 years old, give one to four teaspoons every four hours, not to exceed 24 teaspoons in 24 hours. It is best to try to give the smallest dosage at first to see if your child can get by with less medication.

Missing a Dose: Give the missed dose and then wait four hour to give the next dose. Maintain the new schedule.

Side Effects:

Minor and expected:
• drowsiness

ROBITUSSIN (*continued*)

Serious adverse reactions (CALL YOUR DOCTOR):
- nausea, vomiting, upset stomach

Effects of Long-Term Use: not applicable

Habit-Forming Possibility: none

Precautions and Suggestions:

- A persistent cough may be sign of a serious illness. If the cough lasts longer than one week, stop giving this medication and call your doctor.
- Give this and any cough preparations only if really needed; for example, when your child cannot sleep because of constant coughing. A cough is a defense mechanism and should be allowed to occur if it does not cause undue discomfort.

ROMILAR CHILDREN'S COUGH SYRUP

Ingredient(s): dextromethorphan

Equivalent Product(s): none

Used For: controlling coughing

Dosage Form and Strength: syrup—2.5 mg per 5 ml

Storage: Store at room temperature.

This Drug Should Not Be Used If: your child is allergic to its ingredient. This product should not be used for a chronic cough (such as that caused by asthma) or for a cough that produces a great amount of secretions. You should not give this medication if your child has a high fever, persistent headache, rash, nausea, or vomiting. Call your doctor.

How to Use: Give children aged two to six years ½ teaspoon every four hours, not to exceed 30 mg in 24 hours. Give children aged seven to 12 years one teaspoon every four hours, not to exceed 40 mg in 24 hours.

Missing a Dose: Give the missed dose and then wait four to eight hours to give the next dose. Increasing the dose or giving doses close together increases the action of the drug.

Side Effects:

Minor and expected:
• drowsiness, nausea, vomiting

Serious adverse reactions (CALL YOUR DOCTOR):
• none known

Effects of Long-Term Use: not applicable

ROMILAR CHILDREN'S COUGH SYRUP (*continued*)

Habit-Forming Possibility: none

Precautions and Suggestions:

- A persistent cough may be a sign of a serious illness. If the cough lasts longer than one week, stop giving this medication and call your doctor.
- Give this and any cough preparations only if really needed; for example, when your child cannot sleep because of constant coughing. A cough is a defense mechanism and should be allowed to occur if it does not cause undue discomfort.

SUDAFED

Ingredient(s): pseudoephedrine hydrochloride

Equivalent Product(s): Cenafed, Kodet SE, Neofed, Novafed, Peedee Dose, pseudoephedrine (generic), Sudrin

Used For: temporary relief of stuffy nose

Dosage Form and Strength: tablet—30 mg, 60 mg; liquid—30 mg per 5 ml

Storage: Store at room temperature in a dry, dark place.

This Drug Should Not Be Used If: your child is allergic to its ingredient or has a history of diabetes or heart disease. This drug is not recommended for children under the age of two years.

How to Use: For children aged two to five years, give ½ teaspoon of liquid form every six hours, not to exceed two teaspoons in 24 hours. For children aged six to 12 years, give 30 mg every six hours, not to exceed 120 mg in 24 hours. For children over 12 years, give 60 mg every six hours, not to exceed 240 mg in 24 hours. If symptoms do not improve within seven days or if your child develops a high fever, discontinue using the medication and call your doctor.

Missing a Dose: Give the missed dose and then wait six hours to give the next dose. Maintain the new schedule.

Side Effects:

    Minor and expected: drowsiness, headache, rapid heartbeat

    Serious adverse reactions (CALL YOUR DOCTOR):
- sweating, deep sleep or sleeplessness, nervousness, dizziness, heartbeat irregularities

Effects of Long-Term Use: not applicable since you should not use for more than seven days

SUDAFED (*continued*)

Habit-Forming Possibility: none

Precautions and Suggestions:

- Do not exceed recommended dosages.
- Oral nasal decongestants are usually not as effective as nose drops, but they are active longer and have not been found to cause increased stuffiness.

INDEX

gamma benzene hexachloride, 159–60

Gantrisin, 153–55

gargle, saltwater, 84, 97

generic drugs, 69

GG-CEN, 228

giving medications. *See* administering medications

German Measles. *See* rubella

Glyate, 228

glycerine suppositories for constipation, 106

Glycotuss, 228

growth and development effects of drugs on, 56

guaifenesin, 228

Guiamid, 228

Guiatuss, 228

Gynecort, 214

Haemophilus influenzae B. *See* Hib immunization

Halotussin, 228

headache
    and chicken pox, 100
    as drug side effect, 82, 83
    and vomiting, 103
    when to call doctor, 41, 43, 92 (table)

heart infection
    as complication of strep throat, 96

heat
    to treat injury, 92

herpes simplex vaccine, 33

Hib immunization, 29

hidden side effects, 84

histamines, 94, 96

Histatapp, 147

hot steam vaporizer, 13

hydrocortisone, 214–15

hydrocortisone cream, 108

hydrocortisone, neomycin sulfate, polymyxin B sulfate, and (ointment only) bacitracin zinc, 135–37, 138–39

hydrogen peroxide, 9

hyperactivity, 56

hyperkinesis. *See* hyperactivity

hypothalamus, 91

ibuprofen, 224
    as acne treatment, 44
    described, 34, 35
    how to use, 45
    as prescription drug, 68
    side effects, 44–45
    warnings, 44
    when not to use, 34, 44, 45

ice
    to treat injury, 92

Ilosone, 150

imipramine hydrochloride, 191–93

immune deficiencies
    and chicken pox, 100

immunizations, 29–33
    schedule, 30
    vaccine for common cold, 93

indications of a drug
    defined, 80

infants
    and risks of diarrhea, 88
    and vitamin/mineral supplements, 26–29

infection
    as cause of fever, 89
    of kidney, 96
    of throat, 96
    urinary tract, 60
    yeast, 108

inflammation
    aspirin for, 7, 35
    aspirin substitute for, 7–8, 35, 42, 44, 45